T0316661

Cambridge Elements ☰

Elements in Public Economics
edited by
Robin Boadway
Queen's University in Canada
Frank A. Cowell
London School of Economics and Political Science
Massimo Florio
University of Milan

COST–BENEFIT ANALYSIS

Per-Olov Johansson
Stockholm School of Economics
Bengt Kriström
Swedish University of Agricultural Sciences

CAMBRIDGE
UNIVERSITY PRESS

CAMBRIDGE
UNIVERSITY PRESS

University Printing House, Cambridge CB2 8BS, United Kingdom

One Liberty Plaza, 20th Floor, New York, NY 10006, USA

477 Williamstown Road, Port Melbourne, VIC 3207, Australia

314–321, 3rd Floor, Plot 3, Splendor Forum, Jasola District Centre, New Delhi – 110025, India

79 Anson Road, #06–04/06, Singapore 079906

Cambridge University Press is part of the University of Cambridge.

It furthers the University's mission by disseminating knowledge in the pursuit of education, learning, and research at the highest international levels of excellence.

www.cambridge.org
Information on this title: www.cambridge.org/9781108462938
DOI: 10.1017/9781108660624

First published 2018

A catalogue record for this publication is available from the British Library.

ISBN 978-1-108-46293-8 Paperback
ISSN 2516-2276 (online)
ISSN 2516-2268 (print)

Cambridge Elements ≡

Cost–Benefit Analysis

DOI: 10.1017/9781108660624
First published online: May 2018

Per-Olov Johansson
Stockholm School of Economics
Bengt Kriström
Swedish University of Agricultural Sciences

Abstract: This Element on cost–benefit analysis provides a summary of recent theoretical and empirical developments and summarizes state-of-the-art stated-preference and revealed-preference valuation methods. The Element discusses how to assess small (or marginal) as well as large (or nonmarginal) projects that have a significant impact on prices and/or other economic variables. We also discuss distortions like taxes, market power, and sticky prices. In addition, risk/uncertainty is considered. A novel feature is the elaboration on flexible evaluation rules for reasonably small projects. Conventional point estimates of projects should be used with care, because they typically give biased results.

Keywords: Cost–Benefit Analysis, Flexible valuation rules, Public goods, Value of statistical life, Risk

ISBNs: 9781108462938 (PB) 9781108660624 (OC)
ISSNs 2516-2276 (online) 2516-2268 (print)

Contents

1 Prologue

This short Element on cost–benefit analysis (CBA) has been written by invitation from the editors of Cambridge Elements in Public Economics. It has been a challenging task, not least because of the page constraint. Nevertheless, we believe that we have addressed most issues that are covered in textbooks. We have also added some new results on how to theoretically define a small and an intermediate-sized project. We show that basing evaluations on point estimates might produce results that are less satisfactory from an empirical point of view. Less restrictive evaluation rules based on linear approximations are introduced. An empirical evaluation compares the properties of different marginal and non-marginal cost–benefit rules. We devote a section to the evaluation of large projects. Evaluating such projects is challenging because one often has to work with line integrals; hopefully, we are able to explain how such integrals work without introducing mathematics (except for relatively simple illustrations). We also provide a state-of-the-art survey of valuation methods that are needed in valuing goods when markets are missing. Both stated preference methods and revealed preference approaches are considered.

We have drawn on our book *Cost–Benefit Analysis for Project Appraisal* (Johansson and Kriström 2016). We believe that the current manual could be useful for graduate students in economics and for those evaluating projects and policies at governments, international organizations, and consulting firms. In particular, the manual provides a toolkit that should be useful to the practitioner, particularly since virtually every actual evaluation provides the appraiser with surprises and effects that are not covered by existing "cookbooks." A particular issue that we have been unable to cover more than marginally is second-best theory. There were simply too many important issues, and some had to be omitted. Some coverage is given by Johansson and Kriström (2016), and a review of the development of second-best theory is provided by Boadway (2017).

CBA is based on conventional microeconomic theory. Behavioral economics is a large and rapidly growing branch of economics. Behavioral economics and the closely related field of behavioral finance couple scientific research on the psychology of decision-making with economic theory to better understand what motivates agents. Behavioral economists typically question the neoclassical postulates in economics, in particular those of unbounded rationality, pure self-interest, and complete self-control. Due to considerations of space, we will not consider behavioral economics in this Element. As noted by Robinson and Hammitt (2011), behavioral economics does not currently provide detailed recommendations with respect to CBA. Therefore, much of the advice provided by their 2011 article is to be viewed as best-practice recommendations. Smith and More (2010) are also skeptical of the usefulness of behavioral economics in CBA. A brand-new text is Weimer (2017).

2 Introduction

Stigler's law of eponymy states that no discovery is named after its original discoverer (Stigler 1980). Nevertheless, many trace the conceptual underpinnings of CBA back to the nineteenth-century engineer and economist Jules Dupuit, who, among other things, developed the concept of "utility remaining to consumers," today known as consumers' surplus (Dupuit 1849).

In 1936, the US Congress passed a flood control act introducing an approach to prioritizing projects:

> The Federal Government should improve or participate in the improvement of navigable waters or their tributaries, including watersheds . . . for flood control if the benefits to whomsoever they may accrue are in excess of estimated costs.[1]

---

[1] http://supreme.justia.com/cases/federal/us/313/508/case.html. The US Army Corps of Engineers was heavily involved in the development of evaluation methods. Refer to Johansson and Kriström (2016, ch. 1) for details.

This is the essence of CBA: a project is recommended if the benefits ("to whomsoever they may accrue") exceeds the costs. The Pareto (1896–1897) criterion says that a project should be undertaken only if at least one individual is made better off and no one is made worse off: a nice but not very useful criterion in real-world evaluations. The Kaldor (1939) compensation principle states that a project should be undertaken if winners, at least hypothetically, can compensate losers; Hicks (1939) proposed the reverse criterion. In reality, a project might mean that those who are initially well-off make further gains while those far down on the social ladder lose out. Such an uneven distributional outcome might motivate that individuals are "weighted" according to some distributional criterion, say, income or wealth. (This approach, involving a social welfare function, requires more measurability and comparability assumptions than the ordinal measurability required by the compensation principle.) For an excellent discussion of the theoretical issues involved, see Boadway and Bruce (1984).

CBA subsequently found new applications in the 1950s, as it was applied to various types of public projects in Europe and later on in developing countries. Some of the most important contributions to the development of the foundations of CBA include Boadway (1975), Drèze and Stern (1987), Just et al. (2004), and Lesourne (1972, 1975). A good introduction is provided by de Rus (2010). The seminal Drèze and Stern approach maximizes a social welfare function subject to scarcity and side constraints; it is excellently covered in the textbook by Florio (2014). In an optimum, in each market supply must equal demand. Each policy or project is attributed a shadow price. Johansson and Kriström (2016, chs. 2–3) use a slightly different approach, but they also use point estimates in the sense that a policy is evaluated at a particular point. As will be shown in Section 7.1, it is sometimes problematic to base empirical evaluations on such concepts. We will often base cost–benefit rules on slightly less restrictive linear approximations, allowing us to provide a more general nonmarginal interpretation of a project. In addition, we provide coverage of projects that are so large that they significantly affect relative prices. However, due to considerations of space, there are empirical large-scale applications that unfortunately must be ignored. These include evaluations of large-scale R&D programs, such as CERN's Large Hadron Collider and significant catastrophic events, such as large earthquakes, water-related disasters, and climate change. Refer to Florio et al. (2016), Johansson and Kriström (2015), and Stern (2007).

The text is structured as follows. Section 3 introduces a number of simple cost–benefit rules in increasingly complex economic environments. Although simple, they are general equilibrium rules, which roughly means that the ripple effects throughout the economy are accounted for. We begin by developing rules for the simplest possible economy and then introduce public goods and externalities, including nonuse values (goods and services that are not directly consumed but nevertheless provide value); i.e., various market distortions/failures. We enrich our model by introducing taxes, showing a simple way of handling taxes in CBA, and then looking at the marginal cost of public funds and the marginal excess burden of taxes. A common illustration in microeconomic textbooks is how taxes can be used to deal with a negative externality. We briefly discuss an alternative policy instrument, namely tradable permits and how they can be treated in CBA. Another common distortion treated in the CBA literature is market power. The two most common varieties, monopoly and monopsony, are considered here. Finally, we turn to market imbalances, or disequilibria. Two different kinds of unemployment are explored as well as excess demand in a (factor or goods) market.

In Section 4 we briefly discuss what can be viewed as intergenerational and intragenerational distributional issues. The first refers to how a project changes the way welfare is distributed over time, leading to the issue of discounting. We explore some of the (thorny) issues involved and compare three often-used investment criteria: net present value, the internal rate of return, and the benefit–cost ratio. We also discuss the seminal Ramsey model and the discount rate it generates. We will also touch upon a recent literature on nonconstant discounting, which includes what is usually referred to as hyperbolic discounting. Sometimes capital market imperfections are present. Section 4.2 briefly considers how to calculate a project's costs when it displaces private capital. Thus far, the focus has been on economies with a single representative household. Sections 4.3 and 4.4 bring in multihousehold economies. A typical project generates both winners and losers, and it will be necessary to somehow aggregate gains and losses. We summarize different ways of handling distributional concerns in CBA, focusing on the Hicks–Kaldor compensation criterion (i.e., the "industry" standard) and social welfare functions. We close these sections by displaying how distributional concerns are handled in some leading international manuals on project evaluations.

Sections 3 and 4 focus on small or marginal projects. Such projects are the main focus of most treatises on CBA. Section 5 deals with large projects, that is, projects that significantly impact prices or other variables. In Section 5.1, we present a case where a single parameter is affected in a significant way, and discuss in some detail how to measure the willingness to pay (WTP) for such a change. We then discuss in Section 5.2 a more complicated case where several parameters change, a case which requires the introduction of line integrals. In Section 5.3 we turn to a case where estimates of benefits or costs are transferred from one application to another. This too raises a question of the magnitude of a project. The section also introduces risk. In Section 5.4 a few common concepts and rules are introduced. The final subsection deals with flexibility as captured by the concepts of quasi-option and option values.

Section 6 reviews different methods for valuing nonpriced commodities. The first part of the section is devoted to stated-preference methods while the second part turns to revealed-preference methods.

Section 7 provides illustrations and recommendations. It introduces what might be termed rules for the evaluation of intermediate-sized projects. In the first illustration, rules for infinitesimally small projects, intermediate-sized projects, and large projects are compared by evaluating the Swedish green (electricity) certificate system. In our second illustration, we observe that virtually all authors on health economics employ a definition of the value of a statistical life (VSL) that is valid for infinitesimally small changes in the survival probability. The section introduces a flexible definition that is applicable to arbitrary-sized changes in the survivor probability, hence, is more realistic in empirical assessments. The two final subsections deal with deterministic sensitivity analysis and risk analysis, two important parts of a well-done CBA.

3 Basic Rules

This section introduces some first simple cost–benefit rules. Although simple, they are general equilibrium rules. They also point at both similarities and differences between partial equilibrium rules and general equilibrium rules. We then introduce public goods and externalities, including goods that provide value although they are not directly consumed (giving so-called nonuse or passive-use values).

3.1 Simple General Equilibrium Rules

In this section, distributional considerations are set aside. A single representative household owns all firms and receives their profits. The government may collect revenue from (distortive) taxes or provide costly public goods. Any surplus (deficit) is returned to (covered by) the household as a lump sum. The (indirect) utility function of this representative household/individual acts as the social welfare function. Ideally, we could record how utility is affected by a considered project, but utility is not observable. The economist's way of handling this problem is to convert effects from units of utility to monetary units. The marginal utility of income is the exchange rate that converts utility to monetary units.

In a general equilibrium perspective, one would expect projects to at least marginally affect some relative prices. A first question is

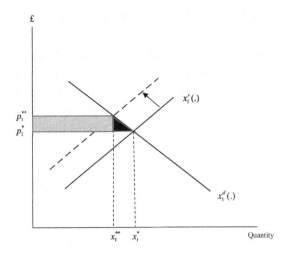

Figure 1 Two market equilibria.

how to handle (infinitesimally) small price changes in CBA. Consider Figure 1: the market is in equilibrium when the commodity price is p_1^*, where the subscript refers to period 1. Suppose there is a small increase in the price of the commodity. The loss of consumer surplus is equal to the negative of the demanded quantity x_1^* times the price increase (follows from [the negative of] Roy's Identity).[2] The gain in producer surplus equals the same quantity, i.e., x_1^* times the marginal increase in the price (follows from Hotelling's lemma).[3] Hence, the changes sum to zero. This means that we can ignore small price adjustments without biasing the CBA.[4] This holds true if other relative prices in the economy,

---

[2] Roy's Identity: the negative of the decrease in utility caused by a small increase in a consumer price divided by the marginal utility of income equals the demand for the commodity.

[3] Hotelling's lemma: the increase in profits resulting from a small increase in the output price equals output.

[4] This also holds if there is a tax on the commodity, but the government's tax revenue is affected. On the other hand, in a company's capital investment appraisal, it is more relevant to include an expected impact on the equilibrium price. Refer to Section 4.4 for the multihousehold case.

including the exchange rate, are also marginally changed by a project.

Now consider a change in the provision of the commodity. Instead of drawing on theoretical properties of the profit function, we choose to formulate a change in profit income in the way one expects the cost–benefit practitioner to evaluate a reasonably small project. If price changes are marginal, a practitioner would look at the following expression:

$$\Delta\pi = p\Delta x^s - \Delta C, \tag{3.1}$$

where $\Delta\pi$ is the change in the (private sector or public sector) firm's present value profit, p is a row vector of present value producer prices, Δx^s is a column vector of quantities, and ΔC is the present value change in total costs.[5] For simplicity, the firm produces a single commodity during a certain number of periods. The first term on the right-hand side of Eq. (3.1) yields the present value revenue; the second term captures the present value of any investment cost plus the present value of the operational costs over the life span of the project (less any scrap value, expressed as a present value but plus any remaining present value costs, for example, relating to the environment). Future cash flows are discounted at the discount rate, and the higher the discount rate the lower the present value of the future cash flows. A profit-maximizing and price-taking firm would set price equal to marginal cost in each period, but it is left to the cost–benefit analyst to empirically investigate whether the firm acts in this way. If not, there are unexploited social gains left because less is produced than what would be socially optimal (ceteris paribus).

5

$$p\Delta x = [p_1 \ldots p_T] \begin{bmatrix} \Delta x_1 \\ \vdots \\ \Delta x_T \end{bmatrix} = p_1\Delta x_1 + \ldots + p_T\Delta x_T,$$

where T is the number of periods. Throughout, any sign denoting the vector transpose operation is suppressed.

The project may also affect the government's revenues or expenditures. Once again, if we focus on the approach one would typically follow in an empirical study, the change in present value lump-sum payments to the representative household is added to the change in profit income:

$$\text{NPV} = \Delta\pi + \Delta m^L, \tag{3.2}$$

where NPV refers to net present value, $\Delta\pi$ is evaluated at producer prices, and Δm^L refers to the positive or negative present value lump-sum payment from the government to the household over the relevant time horizon (assuming there is at least one proportional or unit tax on commodities and/or production factors). Equation (3.2) provides a very simple general equilibrium cost–benefit rule for the very small project. This rule and others stated here can be replicated by working with indirect utility functions and profit functions in a general equilibrium setting.

Because it is assumed that price changes are infinitesimally small, our general equilibrium rules coincide with partial equilibrium rules. However, there is a critical caveat: point-estimate rules such as in the seminal work by Drèze and Stern (1987; see Florio 2014 for a detailed and elegant exposition) and the rules derived in chapters 2 and 3 in Johansson and Kriström (2016) could result in somewhat surprising empirical results. This is elaborated in Sections 7.1 and 7.2. The rules in Eqs. (3.1) and (3.2) are to be interpreted more as linear approximations. The difference may seem unimportant, but as demonstrated in (the more technical) Section 7.1, there is an important difference between point estimates and our linear approximations. For example, even though, say, a change in profits is evaluated at a point, $\Delta\pi$ can be given a broad and nonmarginal interpretation. Refer to Section 7.1 for further details.

Sometimes, one would like to include price effects on the consumer side. This is often the case in transportation economics. For example, a new railway may cause tariffs to be reduced. The most common way to account for this is to compute the net present value via the so-called rule of half:

$$\text{NPV} = -[\Delta p^f x^d + \Delta p^f \frac{\Delta x^d}{2}] + \Delta \pi + \Delta m^L, \tag{3.3}$$

where Δp^f is a vector of changes in consumer prices and x^d is a vector of demands. The rule of half assumes a linear demand curve. In terms of Figure 1, the negative of the first term within brackets in Eq. (3.3) corresponds to the gray rectangle. The negative of the second term within brackets corresponds to the black triangle in Figure 1. The rule of half can be repeated on several subsegments if demand curves are highly nonlinear and/or the price changes are large. Thus, based on this rule it is possible to obtain a more or less exact measure of the change in consumer surplus. Obviously, however, it is straightforward to numerically integrate a demand function between initial and final prices given the currently available software. If producer prices also change more than marginally $\Delta \pi$ should be augmented to account for this fact.

A complication is ignored for the moment: we would like to have a Hicksian (utility held constant) rather than a Marshallian (nominal income held constant) demand curve in Eq. (3.3), but for small price changes this need not be a serious problem. Sometimes, an investigator has access to an econometric estimate of the substitution and income effects, respectively, and can then approximate the Hicksian demand curve. Another problem in applying these rules is that one would have to simultaneously solve for the changes in profit income and taxes, unless the project is infinitesimally small, because π and m^L are arguments in the household's demand functions. Hence, a change in π will affect m^L and vice versa, in general. Therefore, in practical (nonmarginal) applications, the approach is partial equilibrium. There is no way around this problem except to use either a computable general equilibrium (CGE) model or a simulation model of the economy. On the other hand, it is far from obvious how to integrate a small project into such models. (Typically, such models also draw on stronger assumptions with respect to production technologies and utility functions than the approach outlined here.)

Equation (3.3) can be used to evaluate arbitrary-sized projects as long as prices in other sectors remain roughly constant. However, many modifications of the rule remain to be introduced, for example, explicit handling of taxes, market imbalances, externalities, and public goods as well as a discussion of the art of discounting. A fairly straightforward modification regards exports and imports, so let us begin there.

If the economy is open, we could interpret one good as an export good with price $p = e^f \cdot p^{we}$, where e^f is the exchange rate and p^{we} is the world market price in foreign currency. A second good is imported and its price is defined as $p^m = e^f \cdot p^{wm}$. These rules coincide with the "border marginal cost rules" (if prices equal marginal costs) in equation (2.58) in Drèze and Stern (1987). Exports are valued free on board before insurance and freight charges, while imports are valued cost, insurance, freight prices. Within the simple environment considered here, under flexible exchange rates the exchange rate e^f would adjust to clear the current account (the difference between the value of exports and imports). If e^f is fixed, there would typically be a surplus or deficit in the country's current account (implying lending to or borrowing from the rest of the world) that would adjust over time, possibly accompanied by devaluations, revaluations, or internal adjustments in domestic prices relative to foreign prices.

Imposing and modeling foreign exchange reserve constraints (a shadow price on foreign currency) does not seem to be the top priority when designing a cost–benefit rule for more advanced countries. When the world was characterized by fixed exchange rates, more trade barriers, and much less sophisticated international capital markets, many cost–benefit manuals devoted discussion to "pricing" traded and nontraded goods. However, parts of a currency area – say, a country within a larger area or a region within a country with its own currency – might face constraints in capital markets (or nontariff barriers such as quality regulations, standards, etc., which create a wedge between prices across countries). In such cases there is a risk that just about all relative prices are distorted. If so, it seems necessary to work with shadow prices, not least with respect to the cost of financing a new project. Sometimes, though, there are tariffs on imported goods. Such tariffs can be treated in the same way as the commodity tax in Section 3.4: value the commodity at border price (plus any domestic transport cost). Similarly, deduct any export subsidies from the value of an exported good.[6] Refer to Florio (2014, ch. 4.4) for a good discussion of the exchange rate issue.

3.2 Public Goods and Externalities

A project may affect nonpriced goods/services of varying types, such as pure public goods, externalities, or private commodities for which a market is lacking. Examples in this class of goods/services include scenic beauty, bird-watching, fishing, berry picking, hunting experiences, and so on. There is a crucial difference between an unpriced private good – say, berry picking – and a pure public good – say, bird-watching. A pure private good is rival because my consumption of one unit of the good precludes your consumption of that unit. Pure public goods are nonrival because my consumption of the good does not affect your consumption of the good. Such public goods are also nonexcludable for the relevant population, for example, air to breathe in an open area (although air is not produced). However, exclusion may be possible for certain public goods, often termed "club goods"; cable TV provides a simple example. In any case, the WTP for a public good is summed vertically because a unit is enjoyed by all (while we sum demand for a private good horizontally). If we interpret such aggregate WTP measures as present values over the relevant time horizons, they can be added to the terms in Eqs. (3.1), (3.2), and (3.3). Refer to Myles (1995, chs. 9–10) for

---

[6] There are also nontariff barriers to trade like quotas, unreasonable/unjustified packaging, labeling, product standards, and import licenses. Typically, such barriers cause domestic prices to exceed border prices. Hence, society as a whole could save by allowing imports at border prices. A CBA will reflect this fact.

detailed discussion of various types of private and public goods and externalities.

Sometimes, households are assumed to be equipped with (household) production functions. Different inputs are combined to produce an output or experience. For example, the function might be $f^h(x^h, l^h, z)$: the household produces a least-cost trip to a natural park (z) by combining time (l) and gasoline (x) and probably other inputs; the public good appears as an input rather than as a separate argument in the utility function. A public good might also enter the production functions of firms. An example is provided by infrastructure investments, for example, roads. Thus, one can define firms' total marginal WTP or value of the marginal product as a function of the provision of the public good. However, if there is congestion a public good becomes an impure public good because my consumption precludes or at least reduces your use of the good.

The optimal provision of a pure public good requires that the aggregate marginal WTP equals the marginal cost of providing the good. However, if free disposal is possible some individuals might choose to consume a smaller quantity than the one provided initially, possibly zero units. For such individuals the marginal WTP is zero.

We speak of an externality when one agent's consumption or production choices have positive or negative impact on another agent's production or utility (without compensation). Driving a gasoline-powered car causes pollution that negatively affects other people, and possibly also production possibilities (for example, in agriculture). A coal-fired power station creates negative externalities by polluting air and water. Maintaining your yard increases the value of your property and might also increase the value of nearby properties. Beekeepers can collect honey from their hives and the bees will also pollinate surrounding fields and thus aid farmers.

We could treat positive externalities in the same way as public goods; that is, estimate the aggregate WTP as a function of the magnitude/size of the externality. In a CBA of the activity causing the externality, the aggregate WTP for external effects should be added to the activity's benefits. A negative externality could be considered a public bad. Thus, add the minimum compensation needed to willingly accept the externality to the costs of the activity causing the problem.

3.3 Nonuse Values

There is an obvious reason why a commodity, whether manufactured or provided by a natural resource or species, is valued. It simply provides use values, that is, it is an argument in individual utility functions. This is clearly the case for commodities like foods, drinks, television programs, movies, and so on, but the same holds for environmental commodities. For example, a river provides different recreational services like opportunities for fishing, canoeing, and kayaking. The river and its surroundings might provide scenic beauty and other aesthetic values. These values are also consumed and hence are arguments in individual utility functions; such commodities have been covered in this section by the parameter z.

A resource or a service might be valued even if it is not consumed. Such values are often referred to as nonuse values but are sometimes labeled passive-use or intrinsic values. Nonuse values (in a broad and imprecise sense) can be traced back to conservation movements in different countries of the late nineteenth and early twentieth centuries; economists started to look at the concept in the 1960s. There are several different categories of nonuse values, e.g., existence values. The survival of a species or the preservation of a resource is attributed a value. To illustrate, an individual might attribute value to the preservation of a species – for example, the Blue Whale (*Balaenoptera musculusa*), or a building, say a UNESCO world heritage site – even though they will never see or "consume" (experience) one. A person might also positively value the option to consume a resource sometime in the future. This is referred to as an option value, although the term "option value" has a broader meaning in the literature, especially in finance (refer to Section 5.5).

Still another category of nonuse values might be labeled altruistic values. An individual might care about the possibility of others – perhaps in the current or future generation – consuming a resource even if they do not consume it themselves. Or, a person might be a pure altruist in the sense of respecting the preferences of others: the utility function of individual h includes the utility functions of those they care for. If a project increases (decreases) the utility of others this will add to (deduct from) the benefits of the project. There is a risk of double counting benefits (or costs), but this can be avoided if theory is properly applied. In particular, suppose an individual is asked for their WTP in a survey, conditional on knowing that all others pay according to their own WTP. The first individual assumes, therefore, that the utility levels of others will remain constant. Hence, the WTP for "own use" coincides with the total WTP (since others pay so that their levels of utility remain constant).

Altruism might also be paternalistic. For example, a person might be concerned with how a project affects income distribution in society (income-focused altruism) or how it affects health (safety-focused altruism). In such cases the utility functions of others are replaced by the appropriate parameter in the utility function of individual h. In this case, an individual might pay for both their own use and nonuse values plus the impact on others through the change in the parameter. For example, a highway investment reduces not just travel times but also the number of accidents. A safety-focused altruist values the fact that the risk of an accident is also reduced for other road users.

A pure egoist is defined as a person whose utility function only includes their own (and possibly family members') consumption of use and nonuse values. Finally, the pure act of giving is sometimes assumed to provide utility. This is referred to as impure altruism or warm-glow giving. For deeper and more extensive treatments of use and nonuse values a textbook on environmental or welfare economics is recommended, for example, Freeman III et al. (2014).

A project can cause cross-border externalities. For example, airborne emissions might cause damage in neighboring countries. A conventional CBA deals with monetary welfare consequences at the national level. The key question is whether this implies that project consequences occurring outside the borders of the country should be ignored. The answer is provided by the fact that a conventional CBA, just like conventional welfare theory, relies on the concept of consumer sovereignty, that individual preferences should be respected. Therefore, if Britons, say, are nationalistic egoists in the sense that they care only about effects within the borders of the country, a CBA should ignore any effects caused abroad by the project under evaluation. On the other hand, if Britons are altruists in the sense that they care about the impact of their actions irrespective of where the impact occurs, a CBA should respect this fact. Loureiro and Loomis (2013) provide evidence that passive-use (or nonuse) values associated with, for example, environmental damage may go well beyond the territorial limits of affected countries. They estimate the WTP to avoid an oil spill similar to the one caused when the oil tanker *Prestige* sank off the coast of Spain in November 2002. Three countries are included in the contingent valuation study: Spain, the UK, and Austria. The mean WTP is positive and of similar magnitude in all three countries.

One can define present-value WTP terms and willingness to accept (WTA) compensation terms for all these different values and add them to Equations (3.1), (3.2), and (3.3). However, it should be noted that some economists, most notably Milgrom (1993), question that any objective, scientific way exists to assess nonuse values in a way that is suitable for inclusion in a CBA.

3.4 Taxes

Lump-sum taxation was introduced in Eqs. (3.2) and (3.3). One way to evaluate a project is as follows: evaluate consumer gains at end-user prices and profit changes for the private/public sector firm under consideration at producer prices, just as in Eq. (3.3). Then estimate Δm^L, noting that the project, if undertaken by the public sector, is accounted for separately by the term $\Delta \pi$. This term captures changes in tax revenues from all taxed commodities and production factors. This is probably the most straightforward approach to use in evaluating nonmarginal projects and is used in Section 7.1, where we compare three different cost–benefit rules. By contrast, the approach taken in this section replaces Δm^L by its components, for example, how the tax revenue from an ad valorem tax on a consumption good is affected by the considered project. In deriving the basic rules in Section 3.1, it was noted that effects of infinitesimally small price changes sum to zero and vanish from the cost–benefit rule. This result generalizes the case where outputs and/or inputs are taxed, and we continue to assume perfectly competitive markets.

Consider an ad valorem (or value-added) tax on demand. As in Eq. (3.2), we record a change in profits $\Delta \pi$ (the firm could be privately owned or run by the public sector). However, we now have to replace Δm^L with $t^A \cdot p \Delta x^d$, where p is the producer price and t^A is the tax (while any effects related to marginal changes in the producer price sum to zero). In other words, if demand increases by the same quantity as supplied by the considered firm, the good is valued at consumer price; the consumer price reflects the marginal WTP for the good. If demand is completely inelastic, the good is valued at producer price. In the latter case, displaced firms are assumed to produce a quantity such that producer price equals marginal cost. Therefore, in this case $\Delta \pi$ reflects the difference, if any, between the value of the additional goods produced by the firm and its additional costs. Equivalently, $\Delta \pi$ represents any difference between the marginal costs of displaced firms ($= p$) and the marginal cost of the firm under investigation (all multiplied by Δx^s).

Next, consider an ad valorem tax on an input used by the small project. If the supply of the input is perfectly elastic, value the input at the producer price, because it reflects the marginal cost and hence the value of the displaced production elsewhere in the economy as more of the input is supplied. If supply is completely inelastic, the considered project will displace production that purchasers value at the consumer price. In this case, value the input at consumer price, that is, inclusive of the tax.

Labor, if taxed, can be valued in the same way as other inputs. If supply is completely elastic, a project requiring more labor displaces leisure time. The value of such time – that is, the reservation wage – is reflected by the after-tax wage. On the other hand, if labor supply is completely inelastic, the considered project must displace production elsewhere in the economy. And price-taking firms will demand labor until the value of the marginal product equals the gross wage rate plus any social security fees. Thus, in the case of a completely inelastic labor supply, value the project's labor at the before-tax wage rate plus any social security fees.

These evaluation rules also apply in the case of unit taxes. We have focused on extreme cases, that is, completely elastic versus completely inelastic demand or supply curves. In intermediate cases, the handling of taxes will be in between the rules stated. To illustrate, if consumer demand increases by a fraction $\alpha < 1$ of the supply by the considered project, value α percent at the consumer price, and value $1 - \alpha$ percent at the producer price (compare postulates b and c in Harberger 1971, p. 785). More complicated cases arise when there are multiple distorting taxes: in contrast to a lump-sum tax, which is unavoidable, taxes that affect relative prices distort the perfect market economy. In principle, one would have to try to account for changes in tax payments by other sectors. One such case, involving a value-added tax, is considered in Section 7.2.

3.5   The Marginal Cost of Public Funds and the Marginal Excess Burden of Taxes

We have addressed the question how to handle taxes in a CBA of a public sector program. In a sense this is straightforward although possibly very complicated to handle in the real world due to a lack of data and estimates of relevant price and income elasticities. There is also a huge literature on closely related issues like the marginal cost of public funds (MCPF or sometimes MCF) and the marginal excess burden (MEB) of taxes. The MCPF measures the welfare cost of raising an additional pound (£) in the presence of distortionary taxation. The MEB is another kind of experiment where typically a hypothetical lump-sum payment is introduced. This payment keeps the individual on the same utility level as with a proposed increase in the income tax. According to Ballard and Fullerton (1992), one can speak of a Harberger-Pigou-Browning tradition or a MEB-tradition in which the marginal cost of public funds is always larger than unity and a Dasgupta-Stiglitz-Atkinson-Stern tradition or MCPF-tradition in which it may be larger or smaller than one.

Suppose that a lump-sum tax is used to increase government revenue in the presence of distortionary taxes. Then the MCPF is defined as:

$$\text{MCPF} = -\frac{1}{V_m}\frac{\partial V(.)/\partial m^L}{\partial N/\partial m^L}, \tag{3.4}$$

where $V(.)$ is the indirect utility function, and N denotes the government's net revenue, that is, tax revenue less money spent on the project under evaluation. Dividing by the marginal utility (V_m) of lump-sum income (m^L) converts the loss in utility caused by the tax increase to monetary units. Obviously, if there are no distortionary taxes, MCPF would equal unity. The MCPF would look the same if a distortionary tax is altered, but the numerical magnitude would change.

The central issue for CBA is how to apply the concept of the MCPF. It can be shown that all taxes (and subsidies) should be removed from the considered project's costs, denoted ΔC^N. These costs should be multiplied by the estimate of MCPF. It is possible to show that this approach theoretically is equivalent to the approach outlined in Section 3.4 on taxes, provided that we in the latter case are able to estimate the general equilibrium impact on m^L. The reader is referred to Johansson and Kriström (2016, ch. 3.4) for details. The MCPF concept assumes that the considered project leaves all relative prices unchanged; otherwise there would be further terms in both the numerator and the denominator of Eq. (3.4) polluting the concept. This is a restrictive assumption. Hence it seems unclear if it is possible to apply the concept if the project under scrutiny has an impact on prices, however small, or if the project funds are provided by a combination of state, local, and private funds. The concept also assumes that the project's output is weakly separable from other commodities in the utility function.[7] If this assumption is violated, there would be a further expression (on the benefits side) because the project's output affects tax revenue from other taxed commodities. Refer to Gahvari (2006) and Dahlby (2008).

A final issue relates to the relationship between the MCPF and the MEB of taxes. In fact, it can be shown that if an arbitrary tax, denoted t^a, is marginally increased, then it holds that $\text{MCPF}^{t^a} = 1 + \partial MEB / \partial t^a$; refer to equation (3.24) in Johansson and Kriström (2016). The MEB is often estimated using computable general equilibrium (CGE) models. Thus the equality between the marginal cost of public funds and $1 + \partial MEB / \partial t^a$ could prove to be extremely useful for CBA. This is because the result suggests that CGE models could be used to estimate the MCPF associated with different ways of financing a marginal project.

3.6 Tradable Permits

A tax is one option for achieving a target, for example, reducing emissions of a harmful gas. Another option is to establish a cap-and-trade system. In the US, the sulfur dioxide (SO2) allowance-trading program was the world's first large-scale pollutant cap-and-trade system. The most familiar example is probably the European permit market for carbon emissions. A holder of one EUA (European Union Allowance) is entitled to emit one ton

---

[7] $U = U[x_1, f(x^A)]$, where x_1 is the commodity under investigation. Thus, changes in x_1 will not affect the x^A vector or tax revenue from the vector.

of carbon dioxide or carbon equivalent greenhouse gas. Most industrial emitters of carbon dioxide, including commercial air traffic within (but not to and from) the EU, are included in the system. Allowances are either distributed free of charge ("grandfathered") or through an auction but the properties of the grandfathering and auction mechanisms will not be considered here. Other applications of tradable permits include management of fisheries, water resources, water pollution, land use, and taxicabs, but here the focus is on harmful emissions.

The obvious question for the cost–benefit practitioner is how to handle emissions if a permit system is in operation. A glance at some major cost–benefit manuals, both European and non-European, reveals that a number of different approaches are recommended. Some value emissions (of CO2) at the global marginal damage cost, others consider permits as a pure transfer, and at least one manual (the UK's Green Book) value emissions at the permit price. This last approach is the correct one. To see why, recall that the number of permits is exogenous. If a project must purchase permits, the price must adjust so as to induce other users to reduce their demand until total demand equals the fixed "supply" of permits. The permit price reflects the value of the marginal product of the marginal displaced permit purchaser. Recall that a factor of production is used in such a quantity that the value of its marginal product equals the factor price. Because the total quantity of emissions is fixed and equal to the number of permits, there is no environmental cost associated with a project causing emissions; emissions are simply reshuffled. Thus, the social cost is equal to the ruling permit price, assuming that the project under evaluation has an insignificant impact on the permit price. If the project is so large that it significantly impacts on the permit price, one would have to evaluate the area under an inverse demand curve for displaced users between their initial and final purchases of permits. The reader is referred to Jorge-Calderón and Johansson (2017) for further details.

3.7 Market Power

If the small firm under evaluation is a monopolist in its output market, the procedure is the same as in Section 3.1, that is, its output is valued at market prices. In other words, in the CBA what matters is the WTP for the new or extra units of the commodity the firm provides. Thus a CBA signals that the monopoly supplies too little output: the marginal WTP for the commodity exceeds the marginal cost of producing it.

Suppose instead that the firm demands an input supplied by a monopolist. Two extreme cases are as follows. At one extreme, for one reason or the other, the monopoly increases its production by the amount demanded by the firm under evaluation, implying that the true social cost is measured by the cost of the inputs needed in producing the extra units. At the other extreme, the proposed project displaces private demand while production of the input remains constant. Then value the input at market price because this price reflects the WTP of displaced users.

Valuing the cost at market price thus provides a reasonable *upper bound* for the social cost if a supplier is suspected of possessing market power. The marginal cost of providing the commodity provides a reasonable *lower bound* for the true social cost in this case. Although here we are concerned with reasonably small projects, it is easy to see how to generalize the result to a larger change. In fact, this may be accomplished by valuing additional units as an area under the marginal cost curve between initial equilibrium level and the final equilibrium level. Naturally, displaced units are valued as the area under the demand curve to the left of the initial equilibrium. Refer to Figure 3 in Section 5.1.

Consider next the case where there is a sole buyer of the output produced by the firm under evaluation. Now, the buyer using the good as an input has market power, that is, is a monopsonist. The value of the marginal product of the input is equal to input price plus a term reflecting how much the firm must increase the price paid on each and every unit in order to be able to acquire an additional unit. Under perfect competition this last term vanishes as the firm can buy "unlimited" amounts without bidding up the price. The social benefits of supplying marginally more of the input is reflected by value of the marginal product of the input. In the absence of other distortions, the social cost equals the marginal cost of providing the input. Thus the social benefit, the value of the marginal product or the marginal WTP for the product, exceeds the price that the selling firm receives. The social benefits are under-estimated if the firm's sales revenue is used as the benefit measure. In other words, if a buyer of the firm's product has market power, then sales revenue is a reasonable *lower bound* for the social benefits, all else being equal. This case is pertinent when evaluating sectors like the forest sector, because it is sometimes claimed that, for example, the Swedish pulp and paper industry possesses market power (both in the timber market and in its output markets). The case where the firm under evaluation itself possesses market power was briefly considered at the beginning of the section.

3.8 Market Imbalances

In this final section we focus on how to handle market imbalances in CBA. Three cases are considered. Two different types of unemployment are discussed first. Then we turn to the case where an input price (or a wage rate) is fixed below its equilibrium level, hence causing excess demand.

3.8.1 Classical Unemployment

We first turn to the question of how to value the services of workers who were unemployed before the project. If the gains in jobs can be counted as a benefit of the project, its social profitability increases. A possible answer was hinted at when discussing taxes on labor and introducing the concept of a worker's reservation wage: the lowest wage that would induce a person to accept a job offer. The social cost of hiring a person who was unemployed before the project is called their reservation wage. There is no loss of production in other sectors of the economy since the person hired is drawn from the pool of unemployed. Therefore, if there is a social cost, it must be in the form of valued "leisure" time. This approach is often illustrated by a wage rate that is fixed above its market-clearing level. As a result, some workers remain unemployed (or underemployed). If the labor supply curve is upward-sloping the reservation wage is strictly positive and equal to the after-tax wage.

However, this is a partial equilibrium approach. If classical unemployment prevails, laborers face a binding constraint in the labor market in addition to their budget constraints while firms are unconstrained. The binding constraint in the labor market implies that the reservation wage falls short of the after-tax wage as long as the constraint in the labor market "bites." There might be induced changes in other relative prices implying adjustments in production. Hence, the considered project may cause employment elsewhere in the economy to increase or decrease. This last feature illustrates neatly that sometimes there is an important difference between partial and general equilibrium appraisal rules. Also note that if there is virtually full employment so that the employment constraint hardly "bites," then the marginal disutility of work effort converted to monetary units (by division by the marginal utility of income) will be approximately equal to the negative of the post-tax wage rate. Then value public sector project as under full employment.

This discussion suggests that the after-tax wage rate is a reasonable *upper bound* for the cost of hiring labor that otherwise would be unemployed (or underemployed). Unemployment benefits perhaps provides a kind of *lower bound* for the social cost, at least if unemployed workers are reluctant to accept wage offers falling short of the unemployment benefit. However, if social security fees are considered a part of the wage package (as future pensions, and so on) rather than a tax this claim may no longer hold, at least not where such fees are high (e.g., in Sweden they are around 50 percent and the cost of hiring a laborer is at least 1.5 times the wage). In addition, the claim assumes that the project is so minor that "spillover" effects to the private sector through adjustments in relative prices are small. If there are several different labor skills, some laborers might face (classical) unemployment and others might face excess demand. The latter can be evaluated drawing on the discussion in Section 3.8.3. Then the different skills can be aggregated to obtain the project's overall social labor cost.

3.8.2 Keynesian Unemployment

Keynesian unemployment is due to deficient total demand in society: firms operate at less than full capacity because they are unable to sell all the output they are willing to sell at ruling prices. Thus they face quantity constraints in their output markets. At the same time households face quantity constraints in the labor market, as above. Formal treatments of Keynesian unemployment are found in Barro and Grossman (1976) and Cuddington et al. (1984), and cost–benefit rules under Keynesian unemployment and other disequilibrium regimes are derived by Johansson (1982).

Any effect of the project on private sector output must go through one of two channels. First, the project's demand for finished goods will stimulate aggregate demand and hence also demand-constrained private sector production. Basically, the famous balanced-budget theorem is in operation, that is, there is a 1:1 relationship between the expansion in aggregate output and the project's demand for goods. Second, depending on whether households consider (other) private consumption and the project's output as substitutes or complements, private sector production decreases or increases. If it decreases, the social cost of the unemployed hired by the project may even exceed the wage cost if enough private-sector workers are displaced. There could also be situations in which the project has a stimulative impact on aggregate demand. If the project provides a public good that is complementary to a private good (e.g., roads and cars), demand for the latter good is stimulated. In this case, the project causes a kind of multiplier effect that adds to the project's social (but not private) profitability.

This analysis clearly shows that sometimes the partial equilibrium view found in many textbooks is problematic. This view treats all labor employed in a marginal project as coming from the pool of unemployed, and implicitly ignores any effect on employment in other sectors of the economy. A problem with the alternative, "general disequilibrium" view, discussed above, is how the cost–benefit practitioner should determine the net effect of a project on aggregate unemployment. In many instances an examination of the sectors directly affected by a project can give valuable information regarding the nature of market imbalances. In some countries, disaggregated econometric macro models are available and can be used to assess the effect of a project on aggregate employment.

3.8.3   Excess Demand in a Market

Sometimes the price of a good is sticky and below its market-clearing level. This affects the cost–benefit rule because now there is excess demand. This means that purchasers of the good are rationed. If firms are not rationed they will purchase an input in such a quantity that the value of the marginal product equals the price of the input. If rationed, the firm is unable to attain this equality. As a consequence, the market price of the input is smaller than the value of the marginal product.

If the project under evaluation uses a rationed good as an input, the nominal cost of the input underestimates the social cost. Recall that the project must displace other users. These latter users lose the value of the marginal product of the input. Therefore, CBA requires that the market price of the input is replaced by a shadow price reflecting the value of the marginal product of displaced users. If labor input is rationed, it is evaluated in the same way since the activity under evaluation must displace an activity where the value of the marginal product exceeds the wage rate (including any social security fees). If the project under evaluation is unable to acquire all inputs needed to achieve the planned output level, this will be reflected in less output than expected.

4 Discounting and Distributional Issues

The literature on the choice of discount rate in social CBA is very comprehensive and at times highly esoteric. However, there is no consensus on its definition, empirical size, or even its sign. No attempt is made here to summarize the different approaches and their characteristics but good overviews can be found in, for example, Harrison (2010), a nearly 200-page study for the Australian Productivity Commission. Most textbooks on public economics and environmental economics, e.g., Freeman III et al. (2014), include detailed summaries of the different existing approaches. In this section, we briefly discuss how to discount and compare the properties of net present values, the internal rate of return, and the benefit–cost ratio. Section 4.1 also discuss the seminal Ramsey model and the discount rate it generates. The concept of nonconstant discounting, for example, hyperbolic discounting, is also addressed. Sometimes capital market imperfections are present. Section 4.2 briefly considers how to calculate a project's costs when it displaces private capital.

Thus far the focus has been on economies with a single representative household, although discounting has important distributional consequences. In a multihousehold society, there are obviously distributional concerns. It might seem reasonable to base evaluations on the Pareto criterion: if someone is better off and no one is worse off with a policy, the policy satisfies the strong Pareto criterion. The weak version of the criterion requires that everyone is better off. Strong Pareto implies weak Pareto but the converse is not necessarily true. However, under certain technical assumptions that preferences are continuous and strictly monotonic they are equivalent; see, for example, Jehle and Reny (2011, ch. 5). The Pareto criterion is pivotal to most if not all attempts by economists to provide aggregation rules. The problem is just that most projects will not satisfy the Pareto criterion, as some will gain while others will lose. The second part of this section provides a brief summary of different ways to handle distributional concerns in CBA.

4.1   Exponential and Nonconstant Discounting

We have used the term present value without specifying how it is calculated. A present value can be calculated for an arbitrary point in time. The most common approaches are to assume that benefits and costs occur at either the beginning or at the end of a year. First-year benefits and/or costs are discounted by $1/(1+r)$ if they occur at the end of the year, where r is the (real) discount rate, while they are undiscounted if they occur at the beginning of the year. In the former case, the present value equals $\sum_t 1/(1+r)^t = [1-(1+r)^{-T}]/r$ if t runs from unity to T, and multiply by $(1+r)$ if items occur at the beginning of years. In continuous time, the present value equals $(1 - e^{-r \cdot T})/r$, i.e., goes to $1/r$ as $T \to \infty$. If a project is evaluated ex ante, it seems natural to calculate present values "today" or possibly at the time when the project is planned to be launched. In the latter case, all values are multiplied by $(1+r)^F$ or e^{rF}, where F is the number of years or periods remaining until the project is launched. Sometimes a project is evaluated in medias res. Then, typically all past values are shifted forward to the year the evaluation is undertaken, that is, are converted to present values at the time of the evaluation. Such an evaluation (or an ex post evaluation) may be undertaken to examine whether the decision to undertake the project was correct given the information available at that time or to minimize the risk of mistakes in future decision making.

Some projects are *mutually exclusive*, for example, two types of machines that can be used to manufacture a commodity. The net present value criterion can be used to rank such projects that all have a common lifespan, say 30 years. If time lifespans differ, one can replicate projects until one arrives at a common total time horizon. If there are only two alternatives, one with a lifespan of 30 years and another with a lifespan of 40 years, the smallest common time horizon is 120 years. Thus, replicate one project four times, the other three times.[8]

[8] $\mathrm{NPV}^{Toi} = \mathrm{NPV}^i \cdot \sum_{t=1}^{IC^i} (1 + r)^{(-(t-1) \cdot T^i)}$, where IC^i is the number of investment

rounds for project i, T^i is the end or termination date of project i, and IC^i

Sometimes, one would prefer to work with annuities. The annuity is a constant amount of money whose present value is equal to the project's net present value (NPV). The annuity approach provides the same ranking as the NPV-approach for projects with a common lifespan; recall that all annuities are multiplied by the same present value. However, for projects with different lives, the annuity approach fails. This is most easily seen by considering two projects with equal net present values. The project with shorter lifespan has a larger annuity, wrongly suggesting that it is more profitable than the other project.

The internal rate of return is the constant discount rate that yields NPV = 0. It is well-known that the internal rate of return is problematic to use. It could be positive for a project whose NPV < 0. Sometimes there are multiple internal rates of return causing NPV = 0, prohibiting the use of the concept to decide on the profitability of the project. Another approach is to look at the benefit–cost ratio. However, this too is a problematic concept. It is sensitive to the classification of items as benefits or negative costs. In addition, it is sensitive to the magnitude of a project. Refer to Johansson and Kriström (2016, pp. 59–60) for details on the properties of the internal rate of return and the benefit–cost ratio.

The discount rate is often derived from a dynamic Ramsey model, the workhorse model in economic growth. A first-order condition for optimality reads:

$$f_k(k) = \eta \cdot \dot{x}^R + n + \delta \tag{4.1}$$

where $f_k(.)$ denotes the marginal product of capital, η denotes the elasticity of the marginal utility with respect to consumption, $\dot{x}^R$ denotes the relative growth of per capita consumption, that is, $\dot{x}^R = \dot{x}/x$, n denotes relative population growth, and δ denotes the

---

is set such that $IC^i \cdot T^i$ is the same for all i. Alternatively, let the total time horizon go to infinity to obtain $\text{NPV}^{\infty i} = \text{NPV}^i \cdot (1 + r)^{T^i} / [(1 + r)^{T^i} - 1] = \text{NPV}^{Toi} \cdot \sum_{t=0}^{\infty} (1 + r)^{(-t \cdot IC^i \cdot T^i)}$. Thus, the infinity approach simply magnifies NPV^{Toi} by a common constant (because $IC^i \cdot T^i$ is the same for all i).

utility discount rate. The elasticity η reflects the curvature of the underlying utility function. In a cardinal world, η coincides with the Arrow-Pratt-de Finetti measure of relative risk aversion. In a steady state where consumption is constant over time, Eq. (5.1) reduces to the Modified Golden Rule: the relevant discount rate is the sum of relative population growth and the utility discount rate. If $\dot{x} = \delta = 0$, the result is what is known as the Golden Rule, and the relative population growth is used as the discount rate.

In a market economy a profit-maximizing firm chooses its stock of capital such that $f_k(k) = r$ at each point in time, where r is the market interest rate. Thus in a perfect market economy $r = \eta \cdot \dot{x} + n + \delta$; see Eq. (7') in Blanchard and Fisher (1996). Obviously it is extremely difficult to estimate η and δ. Nevertheless, the Ramsey equation has recently been used to estimate discount rates for many European and other countries. Refer to section 10.1 in Johansson and Kriström (2016) for a survey.

For projects that generate costs (and revenues) far in the future even a moderate discount rate means that costs (and revenues) are "discounted away." This has been an argument for using hyperbolic discounting. Strotz (1955–1956) stressed the need to introduce declining discount rates over time, but the first hyperbolic discounting in an economic context seems to be attributed to Phelps and Pollak (1968). It should be added that the term hyperbolic discounting is used somewhat loosely. Some use it to refer to any discounting function that is not exponential, while others use it to refer specifically to discount functions of the form $D(t) = (1 + a \cdot t)^{-b}$, where a, possibly set equal to r, and b are positive constants. This function causes a quite complicated pattern, and it is far from self-evident that a particular future generation is attributed a lower discount rate than under exponential discounting. Refer to Johansson and Kriström (2016, pp. 67–69) for further discussion. Some countries, notably Norway and the UK, use declining discount rates in cost–benefit evaluations.[9]

---

[9] Norway uses 4 percent for years 0-40, 3 percent for years 40-75, and 2 percent for years 75-. UK uses 6 different rates, beginning with 3.5 percent for years 0-30, falling to 1 percent for years 301-.

We should briefly address just how to discount when the discount rate changes over time. Suppose it is 3 percent for hundred years and then reduced to 1 percent for events occurring later on. It might seem reasonable to discount an event occurring at year 200 by $(1 + 0.01)^{-200}$. However, the correct approach is $(1 + 0.03)^{-100} \cdot (1 + 0.01)^{-100}$. Therefore, in discrete time, the present value is calculated as follows:

$$\text{NPV} = \sum_{t=1}^{T^1} \frac{B_t - C_t}{(1 + r_1)^t} + \sum_{t=T^1+1}^{T^2} \frac{B_t - C_t}{(1 + r_1)^{T^1} \cdot (1 + r_2)^t} + \dots, \quad (4.2)$$

where the discount rate equals r_1 for T^1 periods, and then changes to r_2 percent, and so on (and B_t and C_t occurs at the end of period t).

There is also the question of the (optimal) timing of an investment. Consider an investment whose benefits increases over time. If the investment is undertaken today, assume that its benefits falls short of its *variable* costs for a number of years, but then the outcome is reversed. The investment may be socially profitable, provided the alternative is business as usual. Nevertheless, postponing the investment until benefits at least cover variable costs increases the present value profitability of the project. In other cases, the planned launch of a project may be too late from a societal perspective. The reader is referred to Johansson and Kriström (2016, pp. 73–75) for an illustration of the optimal timing of an investment, based on a model borrowed from Dixit and Pindyck (1994).

4.2 Capital Market Imperfections

According to the Ramsey approach discussed in Section 4.1, in a perfect market economy the marginal product of capital is equal to the market rate of interest. In turn this interest rate equals the interest rate determined by the Golden rule or the Modified Golden Rule depending upon circumstances. Nonetheless, there is one aspect to address before proceeding to other issues, namely, how to treat capital cost if the project displaces private investment when there is a tax on capital income. In Section 3.4 taxes were considered. If a stock is affected there is an additional effect to consider. To illustrate, consider a renewable resource. Assume that each unit of the resource stock grows by r^B units each year (in value terms and in a steady state). If this growth is harvested and consumed, the stock remains intact forever. On the other hand, if a marginal unit of the stock is harvested, possibly to become an input in a project, a harvest of r^B units is lost this year and the next year, and so on, forever. The present value cost of depleting that marginal unit is thus r^B/r if the discount rate is r; recall that the present value of a fixed amount, say £1, received at the end of each year or period for all eternity, when the interest rate is r, is $1/r$. Note that in the absence of a tax wedge or other distortion, $r^B = r$ and the direct present value cost is unity, as is the case when private consumption is displaced by our project.

As illustrated above with reference to a resource stock, a unit of capital would also have a return in the future. The question is how this marginal unit of capital would have been used in the future. If it is viewed as perpetual (assuming the economy is in a steady state) and its return is consumed, the present value loss would be r^B/r if the social discount rate is r. Thus the cost of this capital unit would be r^B/r in the CBA. If a proportion a of the project's funding is displacing private investment while the remainder crowds out private consumption the unit cost of the project is

$$C^k = a \cdot \frac{r^B}{r} + (1 - a) \cdot 1. \tag{4.3}$$

Thus, the real costs of a project would be multiplied by $C^k \geq 1$. The discount rate used in the CBA would then be the Ramsey rate, denoted r, derived in Section 4.1. There are other approaches, but since they provide more or less the same answer, they are not considered here. Refer to Johansson and Kriström (2016, ch. 4.5) for discussion.

We provide a simple illustration drawn from the US EPA (2010). The pretax rate of return is 5 percent and the post-tax return is

3 percent, which also is the assumed social discount rate. If private investment is displaced, there is an annual loss of tax revenue equal to 2 percent. The present value of this loss is 0.667, assuming a perpetual annuity, that is, $0.02 \cdot (1/0.03) = 0.667$. The loss of consumption, which is 1, is the post-tax revenue stream of 3 percent, discounted at 3 percent: $0.03 \cdot (1/0.03) = 1$. Thus the cost of raising a pound will be £1.667 if the project displaces private investment. If private consumption is displaced, the cost is 1. The total cost of raising one pound is thus $C^k = a \cdot 1.667 + (1 - a) \cdot 1$, where a is the proportion of displaced private investment in financing one pound of the project. Thus the cost of financing the project would be multiplied by the factor $C^k \geq 1$.

However, we have only considered one possible path for the future use of the considered unit of real capital. There are obviously numerous other paths. For example, part of the return could have been invested instead of consumed. In addition, if the country is reasonably small and has access to reasonably competitive international capital markets, C^k may well be close to one. On the other hand, there are countries that probably have almost no access to international capital markets. For such countries the shadow price of capital might be very high. In any case, it is essential to vary the assumptions as a part of a sensitivity analysis. For example, the US EPA (2010) recommends a shadow-price-of-capital approach similar to the one developed in this section, but there is some disagreement on the extent to which private capital is displaced. Until this disagreement is resolved, a two-step approach is recommended.

As a first step, a Ramsey discount rate of 3 percent is used. In a second step the net present values are recalculated based on a social opportunity cost of capital equal to 7 percent. In most cases the results of applying the more detailed shadow-price-of-capital approach is expected to lie somewhere between the net present value estimates. The European Commission's DG Regional Policy (2014) in its revised manual works with $C^k = 1$ for all member states. It recommends a discount rate equal to 5 percent in economic evaluations of infrastructure investments in states that are eligible for the EU's Cohesion Fund and 3 percent for the other member states.

An alternative approach is to impose a particular distribution for the discount rate (and possibly also for C^k), say, a triangular or a truncated normal distribution. Other important variables may also be considered stochastic in such a Monte Carlo simulation exercise. Refer to Section 7.5 for further discussion of the concept of risk analysis. Still another approach is to extend the Ramsey-rate so as to account for uncertainty. Arrow et al. (2012, pp. 10–14) discuss such discount rates, some which resembles the capital asset pricing model (CAPM) discount rate.[10] According to Quinet (2013), France uses a project specific CAPM type of discount rate in project evaluations.[11]

4.3 Who Stands in Cost – Benefit Analysis?

We turn to the question how to aggregate benefits and costs across households. However, there is a more fundamental issue at stake. Who counts, the issue of standing, in CBA? A first decision a practitioner must make is to decide on the relevant geographical area. A CBA can be undertaken, for example, at the county level, the state level, the national level, at a union level (for example EU), or at the global level. However, except for the global approach, we need to make precise what is meant by "those living in a particular country or region". For example, should temporary visitors be included? What about undocumented immigrants or expatriates? What about serial killers and war criminals? What about future generations? What about aborted

---

[10] Gollier and Weitzman (2010) suggest that the appropriate long run discount rate declines over time toward its lowest possible value. Arrow et al. (2014) conclude that the arguments in favor of a declining discount rate are compelling and thus merit serious consideration by regulatory agencies in the United States.

[11] $r = r^f + \phi \cdot \beta$, where r^f denotes the risk free interest rate (2.5 percent), β measures the correlation between the considered project's benefits and economic activity, and ϕ denotes the risk premium (2 percent).

fetuses? Populations are endogenous and variable over time and hard to define.

In addition, the cost–benefit practitioner must also decide on how to delimitate preferences. For example, Swedes may care about damage on human beings and flora and fauna they cause abroad when importing electricity generated by fossil-fueled power plants, or they may be willing to pay something extra to avoid child labor in the textile industry elsewhere. Should these preferences be accounted for in CBA? In Section 3.3 we did argue that CBA should respect the preferences of individuals. However, this is not equivalent to standing because standing is typically taken to mean the *right* to be included in the relevant population.

An illustrative example is provided by climate change. Typically costs due to emissions of CO_2 caused by a domestic policy are estimated at the global level. Other costs and benefits of the policy are estimated at the national level. Apparently, foreigners don't have standing but how their welfare levels are affected by climate change are accounted for. Refer to Whittington and MacRae Jr. (1986) for a detailed discussion of the issue of standing in CBA.

4.4   Social Welfare Functions versus Hicks–Kaldor

A complete and consistent ranking of social states (projects) is called a social welfare ordering, and is much like the individual's preference ordering. If the social welfare ordering is continuous, it can be translated into a social welfare function. This is simply a function of the utility levels of all individuals such that a higher value of the function is preferred to a lower one. Such a function is often called a Bergsonian welfare function or a Bergson–Samuelson social welfare function.[12]

In its most general form a social welfare function can be defined as:

---

[12] Abram Bergson was the first to use it, and Samuelson is Paul A. Samuelson who was the first American to be awarded the Sveriges Riksbank Prize in Economic Sciences in Memory of Alfred Nobel 1970 and is considered to be one of the greatest economists of modern times.

$$W = W[(V^1(.), \ldots, V^H(.)],$$ (4.4)

where $V^h(.)$ is the indirect utility function of individual h ($h = 1, \ldots$, H). A priori there is not much to say about the form a social welfare function takes, as that depends on who is "behind" the function: it may express the views of parliament or of the reader, for example. In the literature, a social welfare function is generally assumed to have four convenient properties. First, it is assumed to satisfy "welfarism" in that social welfare depends only on the utility levels of individuals, as in (4.4). Second, social welfare is assumed to be increasing with each individual's utility level, ceteris paribus. The function is thus assumed to satisfy the (strong) Pareto criterion, as an increase in the utility of any individual increases social welfare, ceteris paribus. Moreover, if one individual is made worse off, then another individual must be made better off to maintain the same level of social welfare. Third, the intensity of this trade-off is usually assumed to depend on the degree of social inequality, therefore social indifference curves are convex to the origin. Fourth, it is often assumed that the function satisfies the principle of anonymity, in that it does not matter who enjoys a high or low level of utility.[13]

Further assumptions relate to measurability and comparability of utility across individuals. The appendix at the end of chapter 7 in Johansson and Kriström (2016) provides a brief digression into these issues and lists a number of social welfare functions that are common in the literature. Refer to Boadway and Bruce (1984) for a full treatment of the properties of different social welfare functions. In the following, it is simply assumed that the social welfare functions considered are sufficiently well behaved for our purposes, without going into detail.

Besides the Bergson–Samuelson function one of the most common is the Utilitarian social welfare function, which attributes the

---

[13] This assumption makes the Bergson–Samuelson social welfare function symmetric, that is $W = \sum_h g[V^h(.)]$. The Utilitarian welfare function below provides an example of a symmetric function.

same weight to all individuals. In a utilitarian two-person society, the social welfare indifference curves are negatively sloped straight lines. That is, society is willing to give up one unit of Person 1's utility for a gain of one unit of Person 2's utility. This holds regardless of the degree of inequality in society; society is completely indifferent to the degree of inequality between individuals. According to the Rawlsian or maximin social welfare function, society's indifference curves are L-shaped. Society only cares for the worst-off individual.

Let us now use the social welfare function to assess a small project. Suppose each individual pays (or receives compensation) to remain at their initial level of utility. Denote this amount, i.e., the individual compensating variation, CV^h. Then the change in social welfare is equal to:

$$dW = \sum_h W_h \cdot V_m^h \cdot CV^h, \tag{4.5}$$

where W_h is the weight attributed to individual h, that is, the derivative of the social welfare function with respect to the utility level of that individual, and V_m^h is the individual's marginal utility of income; the product $W_h \cdot V_m^h$ is termed the social marginal utility of income of individual h. Alternatively, we could base the evaluation on the equivalent variation, EV, where all individuals are kept at the same levels of utility as they have with a project. In a Utilitarian society, the welfare weights W_h are all equal, and typically normalized to unity, but the marginal utility of income typically depends on income and other parameters. In a Rawlsian society $W_h = 0$ for all but the worst-off individual or group.

Assume that the aggregate WTP in (4.5) is positive, i.e., $\sum_h CV^h > 0$, although WTP may be negative for some individuals. Then it can be shown that there exists redistributions such that some are better off and none is worse off with the (infinitesimally small) project, i.e., are Pareto. The project seemingly increases social welfare. However, this assumes that there is actual compensation. If compensation is hypothetical, some will gain and others will lose, in general. Hence, the sign of dW is ambiguous even though aggregate WTP is positive.

The hypothetical compensation criterion is often referred to as the Hicks–Kaldor criterion (although there are several other compensation criteria).

The Hicks–Kaldor criterion thus "separates" efficiency from distribution by handling over the latter aspect to decision makers. While seemingly elegant, strong, ethical assumptions are nonetheless involved in the criterion, because the proposed project might cause the most well off to gain while the worst off loses. Even if it can be shown that gainers are able to hypothetically compensate losers many would object to the actual outcome. Therefore, we might want to turn to the approach suggested by Eq. (4.5). The problem is that the weights are both extremely difficult to estimate and sensitive to the assumed shape of the social welfare function.

The next question is if the two considered criteria ever coincide. In fact, they do. This occurs if social welfare is maximized because then $W_h \cdot V_m^h$ must be the same for everyone. Thus for small projects evaluated at or at least close to a distributional optimum, if it is attainable, a positive aggregate CV (or EV) implies that the project increases social welfare. The Hicks–Kaldor criterion would result in the same recommendation; the distributional problem is, in a way, solved by definition.

Turning to discrete or nonmarginal projects, a positive aggregate CV is not sufficient for compensation to be possible.[14] This result is known as the Boadway paradox; see Boadway (1974), Blackorby and Donaldson (1990), Boadway and Bruce (1984, ch. 9), or Ruiz-Castillo (1987) for a full treatment. Just et al. (2004, pp. 368–372) claim that they have resolved the Boadway paradox. They provide a graphical analysis of a society consisting of two persons, but we are not aware of any formal proof of the result.

Redistribution is not necessarily costless. For example it might affect incentives in a negative way. Therefore, the actual welfare or

---

[14] If $m^{I1}, \ldots, m^{H1}$ is the income distribution with the project at general equilibrium price vector p^1, in general, at this price vector p^1 income distribution after compensation, i.e., $m^{I1} - CV^1, \ldots, m^{H1} - CV^H$ cannot be general equilibrium.

wealth distribution in a country need not be that far from the constrained optimal one: law makers have designed (marginal) tax schemes taking into consideration possible "side effects" so that the actual situation represents a kind of constrained optimum. Such considerations possibly strengthen the arguments for applying cost-benefit rules reminiscent of the Hicks-Kaldor criterion.

Finally, there are a large number of evaluations of the effects of climate change. Typically, integrated assessment models (IAM) are used in such evaluations. Different assumptions are employed with respect to the social welfare functions employed in such IAMs. Some use simple Utilitarian models while others use Rawlsian models. In effect, Botzen and van den Bergh (2014, table 2) identify 14 different social welfare functions that have been used in what they judge to be the most important IAMs, illustrating that a large variety of approaches to incorporating social welfare objectives can be taken in such models. These functions might also be useful in illustrating the distributional effects of policies that affect a single generation.

4.5 On Practical Approaches

If the distribution in society is optimal, or society has at its disposal means for unlimited and costless redistributions, then monetary gains and losses can be summed across individuals. This is perhaps an acceptable assumption (value judgment) to employ in evaluations of projects that primarily affect groups of similar individuals. In all other cases, a weighting procedure is required, unless hypothetical compensation is accepted as the ethical criterion. Since the weights are not directly observable, there is a formidable problem in assessing the social profitability of a project that affects more than a single person. Some indirect and rough approach must be used to obtain information about the weights needed in the aggregation procedure (and those assessing complex climate changes do add up although their evaluations involve a huge number of yet unborn generations, as is further discussed at the end of Section 4.4). Here, we provide a few suggestions.

In some cases it may be possible to estimate a social welfare function for a particular country. In fact, such attempts have been undertaken. McAllister et al. (1989) and Yunker (1989), for example, have estimated social welfare functions for the US economy. Dolan and Tsuchiya (2011) estimate a function with special reference to health.[15] Alternatively, a particular social welfare function may be chosen in order to show how different distributional considerations affect the outcome of a social CBA. To illustrate, consider the isoelastic welfare function:

$$W = \frac{\sum_h (W_h \cdot V^h)^{1-\theta}}{1 - \theta}. \tag{4.6}$$

If the parameter $\theta = 0$ and the weights $W_h = 1$ for all h, Eq. (4.6) reduces to the simple Utilitarian social welfare function. As $\theta \to 1$ with $W_h = 1$, the function reduces to the Bernoulli–Nash (Cobb–Douglas) social welfare function, while as $\theta \to \infty$, the limiting case is the Rawlsian social welfare function; refer to Boadway and Bruce (1984) for details. In this way, one can also use monetary measures to show the decision maker how different distributional assumptions affect the sign of the CBA; simply replace the general social welfare function in Eq. (4.4) by the different ones generated by the isoelastic function in Eq. (4.6).

Mäler (1985, 2002) has suggested that the choice of compensated money measures should in some cases be influenced by distributional considerations. Suppose that initially, before a reasonably small project is undertaken, society is indifferent to small changes in income distribution. Then equivalent variation, which is based on pre-project conditions, is the relevant measure. On the other hand, if it is judged that income distribution with the project is such that small changes in income distribution would not affect social welfare, then the CBA of the project should be based on the compensating variation measure; this measure is defined in terms

---

[15] Saez and Stantcheva (2016) propose to evaluate tax reforms by aggregating money metric losses and gains of different individuals using "generalized social marginal welfare weights".

of final levels of incomes, and so on. The reader is referred to Mäler (1985) for details.

Yet another possibility is to simply report the unweighted sum of gains and losses in the base-case CBA. In a sensitivity analysis the decision maker might be informed that a positive aggregate WTP is a necessary condition for hypothetical compensation. It is also sufficient if relative prices are left more or less unchanged. If the project significantly affects prices, then only identical quasi-homothetic utility functions, will ensure sufficiency (but then there will be no changes in general equilibrium prices according to Blackorby and Donaldson (1990); refer to Boadway and Bruce (1984, p. 35) for quasi-homotheticity. It seems to be a lost cause, unless it turns out that the Boadway paradox can be resolved, for example, along the lines suggested by Just et al. (2004).

In a sensitivity analysis, see Section 7.4, the unweighted sum of gains and losses is often supplemented by a distributional analysis where gains and losses are allocated to different groups, for example, high-income earners, low-income earners, young people, elderly people, people suffering from severe illness, people living in depressed regions, and so on. This provides the decision maker with a possibility to insert their own social marginal utility of income weights, as in Eq. (4.5). Lorenz curves and Gini coefficients, see any textbook on public economics, might be added to illustrate how a (large) policy change affects distribution in society, assuming, of course, that affected groups can be identified.

4.6 The Handling of Distributional Issues in Three Major Manuals

The European Commission's DG Regional Policy unit's cost–benefit manual (European Commission 2014) recommends a stakeholder-matrix approach that identifies how different agents are affected by the policy proposal under evaluation. The stakeholder matrix presents the overall project in a way that relates effects and stakeholders, summarizing the main economic and financial implications of the project, and showing the transfers between stakeholders and the distribution of costs and benefits. It enables the reader to estimate "net" contributions, by canceling out negative effects with positive effects. It also enables equity considerations if welfare weights are incorporated into the analysis.

The manual also uses a weighting procedure based on a social welfare function stated in Eq. (4.6). The marginal social utility of income is defined as $W_h \cdot V_m^h = (\overline{m}/m^h)^\theta$, where $\overline{m}$ denotes average income, a superscript refers to stakeholder h, and θ denotes the elasticity of the marginal utility of income. The manual also illustrates the marginal social utility of income attributed to high-income, medium-income, and low-income groups for different values of the parameter θ (0, 0.3, 0.7, and 1.2).

The UK's Green Book (HM Treasury 2011) suggests that evaluators should assess how the costs and benefits of each option are spread across different income groups, for example income quintiles. A proposal providing greater net benefits to lower income quintiles is rated more favorably than one with benefits accruing largely to higher income quintiles. In the next step the manual suggests a particular social welfare function that can be used in evaluations. In effect it seems to assume $W_h \cdot V_m^h = (\overline{m}/m^h)^\theta$ but with $\theta = 1$. The manual also adjusts for a household's size and composition ("equalization") since a single-person household on £ 1,000 per month is better off than a two-person household on the same amount per month. The manual also addresses other distributional issues such as a project's impact on discrimination. UK discrimination law currently covers gender, marriage, disability and race. In addition, the government (currently, as of fall 2017) is bound by European law, which, at the time of publication of the manual, covered discrimination only on the grounds of gender, marital status, pregnancy and maternity, but is likely to be extended in due course.

The US EPA's manual (US EPA 2010) does not propose an explicit weighing procedure. Based on academic literature and EPA documents and policies, the manual provides a variety of methodological approaches that may be suitable across various regulatory scenarios. The manual goes on to claim that a clear consensus does not exist regarding the most appropriate methods. Instead, the manual provides a broad overview of options for analyzing distributional effects in regulatory analysis. The manual considers the distribution of environmental quality and human health risks across several populations: those that have traditionally been the focus of what is termed environmental justice: children, the elderly, and minority, low-income, or indigenous populations.

5 Evaluating Large Projects and Handling Risks

In this section, focus is shifted from small to large projects. A large project is defined here as a project that has a significant impact on the general equilibrium of the economy. It could be a single relative price that is more than marginally changed by the considered project. In fact, Eq. (3.3) provides such a case because a second-order Taylor approximation is needed in order to capture the impact on demand. In Section 5.1 we return to the case where a single parameter is affected in a significant way, but now we discuss in more detail how to measure WTP. We then turn in Section 5.2 to the more complicated case where several parameter changes, a case which requires the introduction of line integrals. In Section 5.3 we turn to the case where estimates of benefits or costs are transferred from one application to another. This too raises a question of the magnitude of a project.

In the second part of the section risk is introduced. We will speak of risk and uncertainty interchangeably but implicitly assume that probability distributions are known. In contrast, pure uncertainty is often referred to as a situation where not even probabilities are known. Indeed, the concept of uncertainty was probably first introduced to economics by Frank Knight (1921) in his treatise "Risk, Uncertainty, and Profit." Knight drew the distinction between risk, unknown outcomes whose probabilities (or odds) of occurrence can potentially be measured, and uncertainty, involving events that we do not even know how to describe. In any case, the section surveys some standard ways of making decisions in an uncertain world. Section 5.4 presents a few common concepts and rules. Section 5.5 turns to the concepts of option value and quasi-option value. These are closely related to irreversibilities and flexibilities in decision-making.

5.1 Large Changes in a Single Parameter

In general, the Hicksian demand curve will not coincide with the Marshallian or ordinary demand; for graphical illustration the reader is referred to any textbook on microeconomics or public economics. This further illustrates the well-known fact that areas to the left of Marshallian demand curves cannot be interpreted in terms of WTP/WTA. One exception occurs if the utility function is quasi-linear because compensated and ordinary demand functions coincide in that special case; $U = u(x_1, \ldots, x_{n-1}) + x_n$. The other special case occurs when the change is small or marginal in the sense discussed in Section 3.1. There are attempts to provide error bounds when ordinary consumer surplus measures are used as proxies for their compensated counterparts, the most well-known being the Willig formula. Refer to Johansson and Kriström (2016, section 9.4) for details.

Consider Figure 2. Due to technological development the supply curve rotates to the right. This causes the equilibrium price to fall from p^0 to p^1. Assuming that preferences are quasi-linear, the consumer's WTP equals area A + B. The supplier loses area A but gains area C (and would prefer to not "update" its technology if A > C). Thus the social surplus equals area B + C. If preferences are not quasi-linear, one would have to replace the Marshallian demand curve by a Hicksian or income-compensated one, where utility is held constant throughout at its initial level. The area to the left of this curve between initial and final prices reflects the consumer's maximal WTP for the shift, that is, the compensating variation. No such procedure is required on the supply side because there are no income effects.

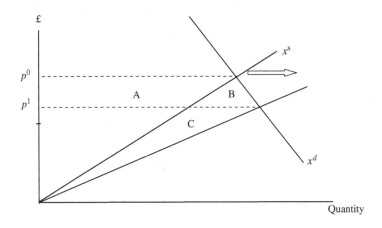

Figure 2 A policy increasing the supply of a good.

We have focused on the compensating variation here. There are other income-compensated measures. The equivalent variation is probably the most well-known alternative to the compensating variation; it is defined as an amount of money such that the consumer reaches the same level of welfare as if a particular project is undertaken. Both these concepts are needed if one would like to estimate the WTP for both an increase and a decrease in a parameter, say a price. If the price in Figure 2 is increased, the consumer is willing to pay in order to avoid the increase. This WTP is captured by the equivalent variation, while the compensating variation reflects the minimal compensation needed in order to be willing to accept the increase in the price.

Figure 3 illustrates the outcome when instead there is a *ceteris paribus* increase in an input price due to an outward shift of the demand curve; the public sector increases its demand by Δx^p units (for simplicity from zero units). The representative supplier gains the area to the left of the supply curve between p^0 and p^1. The private firms demanding the input loses the area to the left of the initial demand curve between initial and final prices. Hence, the area to the left of this demand curve represents both a gain and a loss and hence the areas sum to zero. The public sector pays

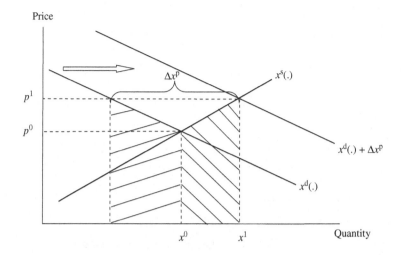

Figure 3 The social cost (shaded areas) of an increase in demand by Δx^p units.

$p^1 \cdot \Delta x^p$. Hence, the "upside down" triangle above the supply curve and between the two demand curves "nets out" implying that what remains are the two shaded areas in the figure. The right-hand side area represents the social cost of producing $x^1 - x^0$ extra units while the left-hand side area represents the value of production that is displaced. Thus, in this case, evaluating the cost function at final prices provides an *upper bound* to the societal cost while evaluating it at initial prices provides a form of *lower bound*. As noted above, there is no problem in using profit (or cost) functions in evaluating large price changes because there are no income effects.

5.2   Large Changes in Multiple Parameters

How do Marshallian and Hicksian concepts perform if several parameters are changed? The supply curve of a private good is assumed to be horizontal (and firms supply whatever is demanded) but there is a technological shift so that the supply curve shifts downward. Moreover, the provision of a public good is increased, once again assuming a constant marginal cost. The combination of these changes is the project to evaluate. Now two parameters are changed, seemingly giving rise to two integrals. Mathematically, they can be written as one integral, called a line integral. Such an integral (sometimes called a path integral) of a scalar-valued function can be thought of as a generalization of the one-variable integral of a function over an interval, where the interval can be shaped into a curve.

We apply the concept of a line integral to the problem just outlined. As affected firms continue to make zero profits, the focus is on a Marshallian consumer surplus change in the private good-market. Add to this change the value of the change in the provision of the public good. There are now two problems in using the Marshallian concept. First of all, as pointed out previously, areas to the left of a Marshallian demand curve do not reflect the WTP. Second, there is a path dependency problem: the order in which prices and other parameters are changed typically affects the magnitude and possibly even sign of the line integral. It does not make sense to have an aggregate surplus measure whose size might range from minus infinity to plus infinity depending on the path taken. Therefore, the interest is shifted to income-compensated or Hicksian concepts. (A necessary and almost sufficient condition for path independency is that cross derivatives are symmetric. This condition holds for both the consumer's indirect utility and expenditure functions as well as for the firm's profit and cost functions.)

Figure 4 provides a graphical illustration. Suppose that the price of the private good is reduced keeping the provision of the public good, denoted z in the figure, constant at its initial level; recall that the (compensated) demand function for the private good typically has the public good as an argument. The representative consumer gains area A in the upper panel of the figure. The compensated WTP curves for the public good are found in the lower panel of Figure 4. The provision of the good is increased from z^0 to z^1 and is associated with a cost as covered by the shaded area in the figure. The change is evaluated conditional on the price of the private

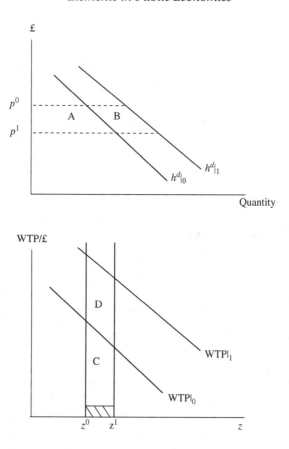

Figure 4 Using different paths to evaluate large changes
in two markets.

good being at its new lower level p^1, that is, as the value of the area below the WTP$|_1$-curve between z^0 and z^1. This yields the value of Area C + D (net of the cost for the extra provision of the public good).

Consider the converse evaluation. Now the surplus in the z-market is evaluated below the WTP$|_0$-curve, that is, p is held at its initial level p^0, yielding the value of Area C. The price decrease in the market for the private good is evaluated to the left of the $h^d|_1$-curve between p^0 and p^1 yielding the value of Area A + B. As Hicksian demand functions have symmetric cross derivatives the integrals/-measures are path independent. Hence Area A + C + D = C + A + B and is equal to the areas obtained if one follows any other permissible path, for example, change both parameters simultaneously. However, the WTP for, say, the public good depends on whether the survey asks, "What is your maximal WTP for ____?" or "What is your maximal WTP for ____, conditional on having paid £A for the lower price of the private good?" The further in a conditional valuation sequence a good is evaluated, the lower is the WTP. The sum of a person's unconditional WTP's for cars may go to almost any amount if sufficiently many cars are involved. On the other hand, working with conditional WTP measures, the budget constraint is respected.

We supply a very simple numerical example. The consumer is equipped with logarithmic Cobb-Douglas preferences. Suppressing constant terms, the indirect utility function is $V = \ln(m) - (1/2)\cdot\ln(p)$, where the price of a second good acting as the numéraire equals unity. By Roy's identity, the demand function equals $x(.) = (1/2)\cdot m/p$. Suppose that both m and p are changed (from, say, 50 to 60 and from 10 to 8, respectively). Obviously, the size of the area to the left of the demand curve between initial and final prices (around 5.58 and 6.69) depends on whether income is hold at its initial or its final level. The WTP for a change in income equals the change itself, that is, equals 10 for both paths.[16] Thus, we arrive at two different amounts, depending on the order in which the parameters are changed. Using the indirect utility function ($\ln(60 - CV) - (1/2)\ln(8) = \ln(50) - (1/2)\ln(10)$), one finds that the WTP, i.e., CV, is around 15.28. (Alternatively, one could proceed sequentially by first changing income and letting the person pay for this change. In the next step let the person pay for the price change, conditional on what was paid for the change in income. Reverse the order and you will obtain the same answer. Or base the evaluation on the Hicksian demand

[16] $dV = V_m(.)\cdot[-x(.)dp + 1\cdot dm]$. Divide by V_m and integrate the right-hand side expression. One realizes that dV/V_m is problematic because both the numerator and the denominator changes as p and m are varied. Hence the integrated measure does not reflect the change in WTP/WTA or utility.

function $h(.) = e^{V^0}/\sqrt{p}$, where V^0 (≈ 2.068) refers to the initial level of utility.)

On the other hand, if both prices are changed holding income constant and acting as numéraire, the cross derivatives of the Cobb-Douglas Marshallian demand functions are symmetric (and equal to zero), hence the line integral is path independent. Nevertheless the areas to the left of the Marshallian (Cobb–Douglas) demand curves do not reflect the combined WTP for the changes; recall that the slopes of these curves differ from their Hicksian counterparts unless preferences are quasi-linear.

5.3   On the Dangers of Value Transfers

Sometimes, a cost–benefit practitioner faces evaluation challenges that are hard to classify as "large" or "small" and evaluations that must be based on multiple data bases. In particular, many different activities and values, use as well as non-use, may be affected. One evaluation approach would be a large scale survey where respondents are asked their total WTP for all changes caused by the policy. Alternatively, we could proceed sequentially as previously discussed, noting that the sequencing has an impact on the reported WTP for an individual category. In theory, at least, the two approaches should produce the same overall number.

If such a large-scale approach is impossible, the analyst could collect data from different sources. There may be a travel-cost study of, say, freshwater fishing in some river that can be used either directly or by adjusting the coefficients and hence the value of the fishing activity could be "transferred" to the actual evaluation. Similarly, there may be results available from a contingent valuation study assessing the non-use values caused by some measure affecting aesthetic and ecological values somewhere in the country. These non-use benefits might be transferable to the study under consideration. This approach could be classified as value or benefit transfer. Obviously, it is tricky to undertake such transfers, because a measure that is correct in one context is not necessarily correct in another context. Contextual differences can include, for example, population, incomes, cultural differences, and so on.

There are several online databases, allowing the practitioner to easily collect data from thousands of studies. For example, the Environmental Valuation Reference Inventory (www.evri.ca) is a comprehensive database detailing, as of 2017, more than 4,000 studies. The Review of Externalities Data database (http://www.isis-it.net/red/) is hosted by the European Commission and focuses on power generation, transport, and waste, while the TEEB Valuation database (https://www.es-partnership.org/services/data-knowledge-sharing/ecosystem-service-valuation-database/) contains over 1,350 downloadable data-points. Refer to Kriström and Johansson (2015) for a number of online resources on nonmarket values.

Returning to our "small versus large" issue, a question is whether the policy really could be considered "small." If so, we could aggregate by simply summing the different monetary items. If the project is nonmarginal, this aggregation would be like summing my WTP for a BMW plus my WTP for a Volvo plus my ___. That is, if the estimates are collected from different sources, we would arrive at a measure that does not respect or reflect budget constraints. This is possibly the most problematic feature of using values from different valuation studies, at least if the policy change is deemed to be large. For an outsider it is more or less impossible to judge whether a particular policy change is marginal or nonmarginal. It is important that investigators address this aggregation issue whenever undertaking empirical evaluations. After all, it is the investigators that have the most detailed knowledge about the sizes of different items relative to the relevant markets. And they should ideally share their "insider information" with outsiders and decision makers.

5.4 A Risky World

In order to be able to say anything meaningful about attitudes toward risk we must assume that the utility function is concave or convex. Concavity or convexity of a function is a cardinal property.

Therefore we now leave the ordinal world, where individuals are able to rank different states, and are equipped with quasi-concave utility functions. As before, focus is often on a single representative household. However, implicitly it is assumed that there is large number of individuals. Typically there are a number of possible outcomes or states of the world. Ex ante it is unknown what state will be realized although we assume it is possible to attribute a probability that a particular state will occur. For example, the probability of rain in London on a particular day may be 0.85.

A risk-averse individual is equipped with a strictly concave utility function, let's say with respect to (profit) income, they prefer the expected profit income rather than "gambling". Strict concavity of the function means that the graph is above the chord, that is, the line segment connecting two points on the curve. A person equipped with an affine (i.e., both concave and convex) utility function is indifferent between the two options while a risk-lover is equipped with a strictly convex utility function, and hence prefers the gamble to the expected income. For the risk lover the chord is above the graph, while for the risk neutral person they coincide. We could establish the same results with respect to randomness in a public good.

The Arrow–Pratt–de Finetti measure of absolute risk aversion is defined as $\eta^A = -V_{mm}/V_m$, where subscripts refer to first and second derivatives of the indirect utility function with respect to income m. The relative risk aversion coefficient is obtained by multiplying by income to obtain $\eta = -m \cdot V_{mm}/V_m$. Obviously, they are both positive for a risk-averse individual since such a person is equipped with a utility function that is strictly concave in income ($V_m > 0$ and $V_{mm} < 0$). The coefficients are zero for the risk-neutral person because for them $V_m > 0$ but $V_{mm} = 0$. Note that these measures are "local," that is, are evaluated at a particular level of income.

Consider now the case where there is no uncertainty initially. Suppose that a project will add to, say, income but in a stochastic manner in a two-state world; with a certain probability it is a "small" addition to income, with one minus this probability it is a "big" addition. Let the household pay for this shift so as to remain

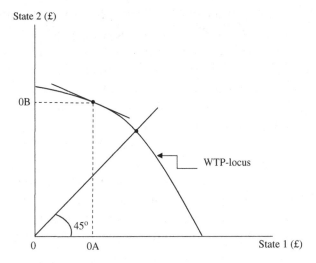

Figure 5 A WTP-locus.

at the initial level of utility. Because the household pays in both states of the world, there is an infinity of payment schemes. This is illustrated by the WTP-locus in Figure 5; refer to Graham (1981) for details. The two most common payment schemes are highlighted. The household may make a uniform payment regardless of which state is realized. This contract is sometimes labeled "option price" but might as well be called a non-contingent compensating variation. It is located at the intersection between the 45° ray and the WTP-locus in the figure. This is a good option if risk is collective (and households are relatively equal), that is, if everybody face the same state of the world. Another possibility is that the contract is actuarially fair and risks are "private" or insurable.[17] Then the payments will reflect the likelihood of different states and the marginal utility of income is evened out across states of the world. This is illustrated by the tangency ("fair bet") of the negatively sloped "budget" line whose slope reflects the probabilities of

[17] For a risk to be insurable, loss must be due to chance; loss must be measurable and definite; risk must both be predictable and not catastrophic; many individuals must be exposed to the risk, and must be affected at random.

the states occurring and the WTP-locus. Then the individual pays 0A if State 1 occurs and 0B if State 2 occurs; this corresponds to a certain or state-independent payment given by the intersection of the "budget" line and the 45° ray. The fair bet is the ideal candidate if risk is insurable. However, there is also the question how costly it is to design state-dependent contracts, for example, in WTP-studies of the kind discussed in Section 6.1.

Let us consider a very simple application. Suppose that the project under consideration involves the provision of a public good. However, there is a stochastic element affecting the marginal utility of the good and possibly also making the marginal utility of income stochastic; for example, the provision of the public good might be stochastic as seen from today. Next, assume that there is a marginal increase in the provision of the public good. The representative household makes a non-contingent payment such that its expected utility remains constant. This non-contingent CV is compared to the costs of the project. To illustrate, assume that the expected indirect utility function is $V^E = \ln(m) + \mu_1 \cdot \ln(z_1) + \mu_2 \cdot \ln(z_2)$, where there are just two states of the world, μ_i denotes the probability of state i occurring, and z_i refers to the provision of the public good in state $i = 1, 2$. Now, let $z = 1$ in both states initially (so that $\ln(1) = 0$), because we know what state has been realized, and set $m = 100$. Assume that the considered project provides 50 percent of the population with two units of z while it provides the other half with only one unit, and the probability that a particular household ends up in either half is assumed to be $1/2$. The non-contingent WTP is implicitly defined by $(1/2) \cdot [\ln(100 - CV_1) + \ln(100 - CV_2) + \ln(2)] = \ln(100)$ with $CV_1 = CV_2 \approx 29.3$. A WTP-locus can easily be traced out: given what is paid in one of the states, the maximal WTP in the other state can be determined. Contracts run from (50, 0) to (0, 50), and the WTP-locus is strictly concave to the origin as in Figure 5. Because income is the same in both states, the fair bet coincides with the non-contingent CV; making state-independent payments evens out the marginal utility of income, i.e., $dCV_2/dCV_1 = -\mu_1/\mu_2 = -1$ in this example.

A slightly different concept is the expected compensating variation (or equivalent variation or Marshallian consumer surplus). In terms of the above example, one defines the maximal WTP provided state $i = 1, 2$ occurs. The expected compensating variation is defined as:

$$CV^E = \mu_1 \cdot CV_1 + \mu_2 \cdot CV_2. \qquad (5.1)$$

The problem in using this concept is that the payments and the marginal utility of income may be correlated; in the above example $V_{mi} = 1/(m\text{-}CV_i)$. Then the product of their expected values does not necessarily have the same sign as the underlying change in expected utility; there is a covariance term polluting the relationship.[18] Refer to Section 7.5 for further discussion. Therefore, expected consumer surplus measures should be used with great caution. However, if risks are insurable, the marginal utility of income is evened out across states of the world. Then the covariance term vanishes and the concept of expected surpluses works.

Another case refers to changes in probabilities. An obvious example is a measure affecting the survivor probability, for example, improved road safety or a new cure for cancer. However, we postpone a discussion of the VSL until Section 7 where we have a discussion of small versus large projects. How to define the (VSL) depends critically on the magnitude of the risk change.

5.5 On the Value of Flexibility

As briefly discussed in Section 4.1, flexibility with respect to the timing of an investment has a value even within a deterministic setting. This section provides further discussion of the value of flexibility. Consider an extremely simplified example. A firm has to decide on its level of production before its output price is revealed. What is known is that price takes on the

---

[18] A linear approximation yields: $\Delta V^E / V_m^E \approx E[V_{mi} CV_i]/V_m^E = CV^E + \text{cov}(V_{mi}, CV_i)/V_m^E$, where E refers to an expectation operator, and a superscript E refers to an expected value.

"high" value p^h with probability μ^h and the "low" value p^l with probability $\mu^l = 1 - \mu^h$. Assuming that the firm maximizes expected profits, it will produce an amount x^* such that its expected price p^E equals its marginal cost. Its expected profits equal:

$$\pi^E(.) = p^E \cdot x^* - C(x^*) - I \tag{5.2}$$

where $C(.)$ is a variable cost function and I is an investment cost. It is assumed that $\pi^E > 0$. Once the price is revealed, the firm's actual profit is known. It is positive if the price is "high", that is, $\pi^h > 0$. However, assume that the firm has a loss if the price turns out to be low, that is, $\pi^l < 0$. If this state of the world is realized the investment is a bad one.

Suppose instead that it is possible to learn more by postponing the investment by one year. In fact, suppose the firm learns whether the price takes on its high or its low value. The firm will undertake the investment if it is high but not if it is low. Therefore, in this scenario the lowest profit is not a loss but $\pi^0 = 0$. This is in sharp contrast to the above conventional (present value) criterion. The expected outcome of the investment, as viewed from today, is thus:

$$\pi^{FE} = \frac{\mu^h \cdot (p^h \cdot x^h - C(x^h) - I)}{1 + r}, \tag{5.3}$$

where the discount term is there because the investment is postponed by one year, x^h denotes the profit maximizing output level, and the term $\mu^l \cdot 0$ is suppressed because it equals zero. This simple example illustrates the value of flexibility. It need not always be the case that it is profitable to delay a decision but the outcome will not be worse under a flexible strategy than under the conventional "present value" strategy captured by, for example, Eq. (3.2).

Thus, if an investment is totally or at least partially irreversible, there is uncertainty about the future benefits and/or costs of the investment, and there is some leeway about the timing of the investment, then the concept of an option value becomes relevant.

There are several definitions available, but the two most common in environmental and resource economics are the real-option value associated with Dixit and Pindyck (1994), and the quasi-option value associated with Arrow and Fisher (1974), Henry (1974), and Fisher and Hanemann (1987).

The quasi-option value captures the value of information, just as in our simple example above. In addition, investing tomorrow might be more profitable than investing today even in the absence of uncertainty, as Section 4.1 reveals. The real option value also captures this aspect of investment. The relationship between these two concepts has been analyzed (in a simple two-period model) by Mensink and Requate (2005). The Dixit–Pindyck real-option value of postponing an investment, here denoted OV^{DP}, can be decomposed as follows:

$$OV^{DP} = OV^{AFHH} + PPV \qquad (5.4)$$

where OV^{AFHH} is the quasi-option value (≥ 0) reflecting the value of information (the difference between closed-loop and open-loop solutions,[19] as explained by Mensink and Requate 2005), and PPV is the pure postponement value briefly touched upon in Section 4.1 in a deterministic world. The quasi-option value is defined as the difference between the net values of postponement under anticipated learning and under postponement without learning (or adaptive learning/open loop planning). The Dixit-Pindyck option value is the maximal value that can be derived from the option to invest now or later (incorporating learning) less the maximal value that can be derived from the possibility to invest now or never. We will not elaborate further on the definitions of these concepts in this manual; refer to Mensink and Requate (2005) and Traeger (2014) for detailed comparisons of OV^{DP} and OV^{AFHH}.

---

[19] Open loop strategies are formulated as functions of time but cannot be changed over the planning horizon, there is no feedback. Closed loop strategies are permitted to respond to the current state of affairs, for example, cruise control to maintain the speed of a car.

Another approach that comes to mind is a decision tree analysis. This approach focuses on managerial decisions, such as whether to drill additional wells or whether to develop the field. It also accounts for uncertainty in important parameters but in a more rudimentary way (typically by specifying the probabilities that the reserves fall into broad classes, such as large, small, or zero). This approach is considered to be somewhere in between a present value analysis and a real-options approach and is not considered here; see Boyle and Irwin (2004) for discussion and Eppen et al. (1993) for a good overview of the approach.

6 Valuing Nonmarket Goods

Economic valuation methods for non-market goods and services comprise a range of empirical approaches to estimate a monetary value for the trade-off a person would be willing to make to increase the amount or the quality of a good or service for which there exists no market. After a period of more than fifty years of improvement, the approaches have reached a certain degree of maturity and professional acceptance; for example, they are routinely used in US court cases as a starting point for oil-spill damage assessments (which can run into several billions of US dollars). There are probably more than 10,000 papers published, covering a range of issues about economic valuation methods.

While environmental and health studies dominate, an increasing number of applications appear in, inter alia, cultural economics. Since the number of things people care about is virtually without limits, the set of applications for measuring these types of trade-offs is very large. We will divide our exposition into two parts, covering the most used stated-preference and revealed-preference methods.

The stated-preference methods are based on what respondents' state in interviews/questionnaires, generally targeting a person's choices for a proposed change in a well-defined object of choice (such as one's health status or some aspect of environmental quality). Revealed-preference methods uses information on what consumers have been observed choosing in a market related to the non-market good/service. We will discuss travel cost and hedonic pricing, two of the most common methods in this class. Both have a strong grounding in welfare theory. This holds true also for two other methods covered here: those drawing on the concept of weak complementarity and household production functions, respectively. We will not cover averting behavior, an approach that uses expenditures on ways to reduce the impact of a certain negative externality. For example, installing better insulation and triple pane windows can be a way for the household to reduce indoor noise. Thus, the expenditures on such equipment can be assumed to be related to the value of reducing noise. Another approach, value or benefit transfer, was briefly considered in Section 5.3 and is not further considered here. There are several other approximate methods, with little or no grounding in welfare theory, which we skip here.

6.1 Contingent Valuation

The contingent valuation method derives its name from the fact that a valuation question is conditional on the design of the hypothetical market. Carson (2012) provides a comprehensive and authoritative introduction to the large and growing literature on contingent valuation. It includes entries on over 7,500 contingent valuation papers and studies from over 130 countries. The classic approach is to ask an open-ended question, i.e., asking a person for their WTP for a proposal. The (positive or negative) WTP for a change in the provision of a public good, denoted z, holding prices and income constant is defined as follows:

$$V^h(p, m^h - CV, z^1) = V^h(p, m^h, z^0). \tag{6.1}$$

CV is a payment (compensation) if z increases (decreases). In order to define the WTP (or WTA) for changes in both directions the equivalent variation must be added. In both cases, the approach can easily be generalized to cover large and complex projects affecting possibly all relative prices. Any change in lump-sum income could be interpreted as reflecting the proposal's costs.

An alternative is to base the evaluation on a closed-ended format. Now, each respondent is asked whether they are willing to pay a pre-specified amount of money in exchange for a policy. Typically, there is a Yes option and a No option, but a "Don't know" option might be added. The bid is varied across subsamples, and each respondent might constitute a subsample. A respondent votes Yes (No) if the policy increases (decreases) utility. In order to estimate the mean (or median) WTP some randomness must be added. Now, the bid is accepted provided:

$$\Delta V^h = v(p, m^h - a^h, z^1) - v(p, m^h, z^0) + \mu^h > 0, \tag{6.2}$$

where μ^h is a stochastic variable whose mean equals zero. On average the investigator is right but in the individual case they are wrong due to unobservable and seemingly random variations in tastes and other factors.

In contrast to the open-ended approach, the closed-ended approach might seem to require econometric tools in order to arrive at an estimate of the mean (or median) WTP. However, a simple nonparametric approach is often useful as a first rough approximation, based on Ayer et al. (1955). The proportion of "Yes" answers is plotted against bid size, an approach that can be used for WTA experiments as well, but the interpretation of a "Yes" answer is then, of course, different. If the curve is monotonic in the bids, this yields a maximum likelihood estimate of points, the number of points being equal to the number of bids on the underlying distribution function. If the curve is not monotonic, the procedure is repeated using the algorithm of Ayer et al. (1955). This algorithm now has many variants that are more stable, but we will not go into the details here. The monotonic curve is a kind of demand curve for the policy (if bids are on the vertical axis and the proportion of "Yes" answers is plotted on the horizontal axis). Integrating or using some simpler approach to estimate the area under the demand curve (or the survivor function as further explained below) yields an estimate of the mean WTP for the policy, here Δz. This parallels the approach used in measuring WTP as an area under a demand curve. The same technique can be used in the case of open-ended data in order to illustrate how WTP is distributed across the sample.

Another approach is to assume a distribution for μ^h. To look at an area under a "demand curve", the survivor function is used. Probably the most common distribution used in WTP-experiments is the logistic one:

$$G(a) = \frac{1}{1 + e^{-\Delta v}}, \tag{6.3}$$

where $G(.)$ refers to the survivor function, and $\Delta v = v_z \Delta z - v_m \Delta a$. Thus, Δv is a linear approximation of the welfare change in Eq. (6.2). Equation (6.3) has the property that it goes to unity as the bid, i.e. Δa, goes to minus infinity and to zero as the bid goes to plus infinity. Therefore, the mean is obtained by integrating $G(a)$ from zero to ∞, and $1 - G(a)$ from $-\infty$ to 0, and equals v_z/v_m, as is seen by setting $\Delta v = 0$ so that $v_z \Delta z = v_m \Delta a$. Suppose instead that $\Delta v = v_z \Delta z - \beta \cdot \ln(a) \Delta a$. In this case, negative bids are ruled out, but the mean becomes quite involved. Refer to Johansson and Kriström (2016, ch. 9.1) for details. Sometimes it is reasonable to rule out negative bids but also assume that a discrete proportion of respondents has a zero WTP for the policy, that is, there is a "spike" in the distribution.

In recent years there has been an "explosion" in the number of variations in the valuation format. For example, an early variation is the double-bounded format, where a follow-up question is asked. If the respondent accepts (rejects) the first bid, the second bid is increased (decreased). The problem with this approach is the phrasing of the follow-up question; if I have been promised the project for £10 (and I accepted), why should I be asked about paying £20? Probably the most popular approach today is a payment card that allows for uncertainty. In this format, the respondent is asked to consider suggested costs along with the respondent's own assessment about how likely it is that they will pay the chosen amount; Mahieu et al. (2014) provide a recent survey of applications with this approach. A problem with the approach is how to interpret a respondent's uncertainty. To overcome this and other problems, self-selected intervals have been proposed, refer to Belyaev and Kriström (2015).

Johnston et al. (2017) provide contemporary guidance for stated preference studies. They intend to provide a set of guidelines for SP studies that is more comprehensive than that of the original National Oceanic and Atmospheric Administration (NOAA) Blue Ribbon Panel on contingent valuation (Arrow et al. 1993), is more germane to contemporary applications, and reflects the two decades of research since that time.

6.2 Discrete Choice Experiments

Discrete choice experiments are becoming more popular in non-market valuation, and are quite similar to conjoint analysis, popular in marketing. There is a plethora of names in use, e.g. choice experiments, but we will stick with 'discrete choice experiments' here. At any rate, conjoint analysis focuses on the properties of a single good, say a single credit card. The theory underlying conjoint analysis, known as conjoint measurement (a mathematical method for the construction of measurement scales for objects with multiple attributes), was developed by Luce and Tukey (1964). A discrete choice experiment, on the other hand, typically involves several alternatives and the option to opt out or not choose any of the offered alternatives; for example, respondents might choose between different credit cards with different properties (annual fee, credit limit, and so on) or choose no credit card. Useful comparisons between the two approaches are in Gustafsson et al. (2007) and Louviere et al (2010).

Applications began to expand rapidly in marketing in the 1970s; more recently the discrete choice approach has become quite popular in environmental economics, health economics, and transport economics. Many economists see discrete choice experiments as a serious challenger to contingent valuation, but it relies on a different set of elicitation formats and analytical approaches.

Conjoint analysis and discrete choice experiments are techniques for establishing the relative importance of different attributes in the provision of a good. They assume that any good can be defined as a combination of levels of a given set of attributes. The utility derived from the good is thereby determined by the utility of each of the attributes.

There are, typically, five steps in a conjoint analysis (and discrete choice experiments). The first step is to establish the attributes. For example, if the good is a hip protector, its attributes might be its protective effect, ease of handling, comfort, and cost. The next step is to assign levels to the attributes. If all attributes are assigned three levels and there are four attributes, in total there are 81 scenarios. Obviously, we cannot confront a respondent with so many alternatives, so the third step is to select scenarios. Using software (drawing on the linearity assumption, further discussed in what follows), the number can be reduced. These could be split into several lists featuring a different sequence to avoid respondents' boredom. The fourth step is to establish preferences. One possibility is to ask respondents to indicate "Buy" or "Don't buy." Then, the dependent variable is binary. Alternatively, studies might ask respondents to rank each profile (typically on a scale of one (very bad) to seven (very good). One can also use graded pair questions to evaluate two or more programs, where the scale might run from one (the first program is much better) to seven (the second program is much better). Several other ways of establishing preferences are also available. The fifth and final step is to estimate utility. Each of these steps contain a myriad of challenges and we barely scratch the surface of a very extensive literature in economics, statistics and psychology; a few references are provided below.

A pivotal assumption employed in most empirical studies is that utility is linear in each argument. Therefore, the conditional indirect utility function is linear:

$$V^{hj} = v^{hj} + \varepsilon^{hj} = a \cdot p + V_m \cdot (m^h - a^j) + g \cdot A^j + \varepsilon^{hj} \qquad (6.4)$$

where V^{hj} is the utility individual h derives from alternative j, v^{hj} is the part of the utility function that can be "observed" by the investigator, ε^{hj} is a random individual — or profile — specific component providing the randomness necessary for econometric estimation, a is a vector of coefficients, a^j is the price individual h pays for alternative j, and g is a vector of coefficients associated with the attributes of alternative j, that is, A^j. The expected value of the random term is zero, that is, on average the investigator is assumed to be right.

Alternative j is chosen if and only if it provides higher utility than all other alternatives. Two of the most common econometric techniques used to estimate Eq. (6.4) are the logit model and the probit model. Once Eq. (6.4) has been estimated the marginal WTP for changes in the attributes is calculated as:

$$\text{MWTP}_{\Delta A} = \frac{g \cdot \Delta A}{V_m} \qquad (6.5)$$

Because utility, by assumption, is linear in attributes, the marginal WTP can be scaled to fit a change in an attribute of any size. However, this is a highly questionable assumption, and possibly the main weak point of the approach. There are few other applications in which economists willingly postulate linear utility functions. A related problem is to transfer or translate MWTP so as to fit an actual project, for example, how to use data from the hip protector study to generate a hypothesis about the WTP for actual hip protectors. By contrast, in a closed-ended WTP experiment respondents would accept/reject paying a specified amount of money for a *particular* product, say, a well-defined hip protector. In addition, in many cases there is no obvious status quo or without-project option (or an option to abstain from choice). A further problem is that there is no established or uniform way of selecting attributes, their levels, or the way preferences are established. In fact, approaches vary widely among studies. This makes it very difficult to compare different studies. For a detailed, and critical, exposition of discrete choice experiments, focusing on the many assumptions needed, see Kriström and Laitila (2003). For an excellent discussion of the (often lack of) incentive compatibility of different survey formats (contingent valuation as well as discrete choice experiments), refer to Carson and Groves (2007, 2011).

6.3 The Travel-Cost Method

In this section, the travel-cost model is briefly presented. In essence this was the approach suggested by the ingenious economist and statistician Harold Hotelling to the Director of the US National Park Service in 1947; see Hotelling (1949). The Director had asked a number of economists to value a national park. In his letter, Hotelling noted that people travel considerable distances and hence incur travel costs. He goes on to describe how these cost figures can be used to estimate the aggregate consumer surplus in the way suggested below. This might give the impression that the approach is applicable primarily in evaluating recreational sites. However, the basic idea underlying modern approaches to travel demand is that travel is the result of choices that are made by individuals or collective units such as households. The most common discrete choice method in travel forecasting (say, number of people traveling by aircraft, car, or coach from A to B) is the logit model discussed below. An example is provided by the development of logit models for forecasting nationwide intercity travel demand in a country.

In a highly simplified (continuous) case there is a demand function for trips $x^T = x^T(p, m, p^T)$, where p^T is the price of a trip. Therefore, it is possible to estimate consumer surplus as the area to the left of the demand curve between the choke price, where demand goes to zero, and the actual total travel cost. This area represents the value of the activity above actual cost $p^T \cdot x^T$. It might be added that if a cost for time spent at the site is included, the demand curve is shifted upward. If it is a parallel shift, the total consumer surplus is unchanged, otherwise it is affected. A refinement would be to consider a Hicksian demand function because such a function can be used to estimate the

WTP (or WTA compensation if the quality of the activity diminishes); recall the discussion of the shortcomings of ordinary or Marshallian consumer surplus measures in Section 5.1. The earliest travel-cost studies, dating back to the 1960s, used zonal/seasonal data. The idea was to identify zones around the site and travel costs from each zone to the site. Given an estimate of the proportion of those living in a zone that visit the site, we can run a regression relating the proportion of visitors to distance and hence travel cost to the site. Other variables such as costs of reaching substitute sites and socioeconomic conditions (age, gender, income, and so on) might also be included in such regression analysis. Early applications used continuous functional forms, for example, linear or log-linear forms. More recently, count data models have become popular. These models can handle non-negative integers (and in the real world, one would typically make 0, 1, 2, etc. trips).[20] Typically, in the first step a binomial probability model directs the binary outcome of whether a count variable has a value of zero or a positive value; in particular, in a sample there might be many zeros as only a small fraction can be expected to visit the site under examination. In the second step, conditional on a decision to visit the site, the number of visits is estimated. Parsons (2013) provides a good overview of this approach.

Currently, the most popular approach draws on McFadden's random utility maximization (RUM) model. It is a single occasion (say, a day) approach where the individual can choose between visiting a number of different sites. The utility attained depends on the cost of visiting a site and its attributes. The site yielding the highest utility is picked. Site utility for individual h at site i is assumed to be given by:

---

[20] A simple example is provided by the Poisson model, whose density function is $f(x^T = k) = e^{-\gamma}\gamma^k/k!$, $k = 0, 1, \ldots, \infty$. To ensure non-negative probabilities, the expected number of trips can be parameterized as $\gamma = e^{\beta_0 + \beta_p \cdot p^T + \beta \cdot S}$, the β's refer to coefficients and S is a vector of attributes.

$$U^{hi} = \beta_p \cdot p^{Thi} + \beta \cdot z_i + \varepsilon_{hi}, \tag{6.6}$$

where z_i is a vector of attributes (with $i = 1, \ldots, J$). Individual characteristics do not enter as they net out, that is, are identical across sites. However, they might enter if interacted with site characteristics. Also note that β_p is (the negative of) the assumed-constant marginal utility of income in this simple model; trip cost is borne out of lump-sum income. It is often assumed that the error terms ε_{hi} are independently and identically distributed Type 1 extreme value random variables. This gives a multinomial logit for the choice probabilities.

The parameters are estimated using data on actual site choices. Using the estimate for β_p one can obtain consumer surplus estimates (but if the model is nonlinear in trip cost, there is no closed-form solution, implying that numerical methods are used to calculate utility gains). There are also approaches allowing one to go from "daily" trips to seasonal estimates. The latter estimates generally have more policy relevance. The reader is referred to Parsons (2013) for a brief overview of these quite technical issues.

The most recent approach is to estimate Karush–Kuhn–Tucker conditions. In contrast to the Lagrange approach, the Karush–Kuhn–Tucker approach allows for corner solutions. Obviously, this is a much more general approach than the previous ones. A main advantage is the clear link to utility theory. In applying the Karush–Kuhn–Tucker model, it is assumed that individual preferences are randomly distributed in the population. By specifying a parametric form for the consumers' direct utility function, standard Karush–Kuhn–Tucker conditions can be used to identify the participation and site selection probabilities needed to estimate preferences and construct welfare measures. A reason for the few applications of this method is computational complexity, but this is becoming less of an issue. For a brief overview of the Karush–Kuhn–Tucker conditions approach, refer to Parsons (2013).

6.4   Hedonic Methods

The hedonic approach was introduced by Griliches (1971) and Rosen (1974), drawing on the utility theory of Lancaster (1966, 1971), although hedonic regression applied to price index measurement dates back at least to the 1930s. Rosen presented a model of product differentiation based on the hedonic hypothesis that goods are valued for their utility-bearing attributes or characteristics. Hedonic prices are defined as the implicit prices of attributes and are revealed to economic agents from observed prices of differentiated products and the specific amounts of characteristics associated with them. The approach has many applications. As mentioned, it is used to refine consumer and other price indices, and to estimate demand for trips, as well as for studies of automotive and consumer durables markets. Using data on wages and workplace risks it is also used to estimate the VSL.

Rosen's model integrates both the demand and supply side of the market and suggests a way of disentangling the value of the attributes. In his model, consumers consider different houses (described by their characteristics) and select one that is optimal, given preferences and income. Landlords (the suppliers) offer houses with different characteristics so as to maximize profits, given the cost of supplying houses of different type. A hedonic equilibrium is interpreted as a matching between buyers and sellers, such that buyers cannot increase utility by making another choice, and landlords cannot increase profits by supplying another type of house. An important feature of the model is that the household's budget constraint is nonlinear; the price of an attribute varies with the levels of all attributes. This constraint complicates the analysis considerably. Important assumptions behind this model include free mobility, perfect information, and no market power. Rosen suggests a two-step procedure that entails first regressing the price of a differentiated product, say a house, against house attributes and pertinent area characteristics considered affecting the market price, including the attribute of interest for valuation. The estimated price function is then differentiated with respect to the parameter of interest, often air quality. These so-called marginal effects are subsequently used in a second regression on attributes and demand shifters. In this way one can get a function that describes marginal WTP, as a function of income and other pertinent variables. The first stage is now part of the standard toolbox, and the one that is typically used, while the second stage remains an area of active research. The second stage creates a number of issues, mainly from an econometric point of view regarding identification. A key difficulty is that prices are implicit, not explicit, as in traditional market models in which goods are homogenous.

A significant portion of the modern literature on the hedonic method (for non-market valuation) has tried to make progress on the endogeneity/identification problems. We can only sketch a few developments here. One line of research begins with the location decision and the way households "sort" into different neighborhoods leading to the development of certain RUM-models briefly described in Johansson and Kriström (2016). Another approach to address the econometric problems is a regression discontinuity design, a quasi-experimental approach that has its roots in evaluating educational programs. It uses a threshold ("cut-off value"), e.g. a test score, to assign studied objects into treatment groups. An illustrative paper of this approach in hedonics is Chay and Greenstone (2005) who use US data at the county level (N=998, T=1970-1980) on TSP (Total Suspended Particles) and house prices. They study amendments to the Clean Air Act and obtain the "cut-off" value from a threshold given by the EPA, that divided counties into "attainment" and "non-attainment" types. Counties just above the cut-off were more heavily regulated than those just below it, the control group. In this ingenious way, they can construct an exogenous variable that indicates a reduction of TSP and is uncorrelated with house prices. Indeed, regressing house price on TSP, the standard hedonic approach, is vulnerable to endogeneity issues. We refer to Chay and Greenstone (2005) for details of their procedure and a nice review of the econometric problems in hedonic studies. Later contributions have tried to relax some of the assumptions they employed (e.g. by using data on individual houses, rather than county data). Finally, we refer to Coelli et al. (1991) for a CBA involving hedonic pricing.

6.5 Weak Complementarity and Household Production Functions

A major drawback of travel-cost and hedonic models is that they cannot capture non-use values. This is because such values leave no "fingerprint" in the markets. In particular, in some applications, such as environmental policies and health policy issues, this is a serious drawback. Here, we will consider two market-based approaches that possibly are able to capture some non-use values.

The first draws on weak complementarity, introduced by Mäler (1974). Increases in a nonmarketed quality attribute is assumed not to increase utility unless the private good serving as the weak complement is consumed. Moreover, this private commodity must be non-essential, that is, a commodity such that any bundle including the commodity can be matched by a bundle excluding the commodity. A simple example is provided by the utility function $U(.) = \ln(x) + \ln(x_1 + 1) \cdot z$, where z denotes a quality attribute of x_1. The commodity x is essential in the sense that utility tends to minus infinity as x approaches zero from the positive side (0+) regardless of how much of the other commodity is consumed. The second commodity, x_1, is non-essential in the sense that the individual can derive a positive level of utility even if $x_1 = 0$. Moreover, the utility function in question is such that the level of the quality attribute z does not matter when x_1 is not consumed.

Consider a change of the attribute's quality. The quality change can be valued as the difference between two areas to the left of compensated demand curves for the priced commodity x_1 between the choke price and the ruling market price.[21] Thus in certain cases

---

[21] A very simple example is provided by $U = x + z \cdot \ln(x_1+1)$, resulting in $x_1 = h_1 = z/p_1 - 1$. Set the ruling p_1 to 1, $z^0 = 5$, and $z^1 = 10$. Integrate x_1 up to choke prices

it is possible to use market prices to value changes in an attribute or commodity that is not priced in markets. Note that we refrain from a measure based on ordinary or Marshallian demand functions. The reason is that both a price and quality are changed, implying that there might be a path dependency problem if the analysis is based on Marshallian concepts, as was shown in Section 5.2. Refer to Palmquist (2005) for a detailed treatment.

A variation of this approach is to assume that a good or service is produced using a priced private good or service and a public good as inputs. For example, the individual might produce trips using a car (x_1) and a road (z) as inputs. In this case, the utility function could be stated as:

$$U = U[\mathrm{X}, f(x_1, z)], \tag{6.7}$$

where $Z = f(x_1, z)$ is the good or service produced, and $f(.)$ is a well-behaved household production function. From the point of view of the individual, the supply of the public good z is fixed. Hence if z is reduced, the individual could "counteract" by buying more of x_1, a reaction often termed averting behavior. If the utility function (6.7) is maximized subject to the usual budget constraint, the demand function for Z can be derived and defined as $Z = Z(\mathrm{P}, p_1, m, z)$. Given that the production function is known, it is straightforward to use the demand function to calculate the marginal WTP for the public good z. In general, however, the functional form of the household production function is unknown. However, by making assumptions about some broad characteristics of the production function, such as whether an input is essential or not or whether two inputs are complements or substitutes, it is possible to calculate the marginal WTP for the public good from market data. The kind of household production function introduced here dates back to Becker (1960) who used a production function approach to model the quality of children, which is produced by inputs of goods and parental time. For the definitive treatment of the approach, refer to Smith (1991).

(5 and 10 respectively) to obtain 14.03 – 4.05. Or use the indirect utility function $V = m + p_1 - z + z \cdot \ln(z/p_1)$ to estimate CV (≈ 9.98) of the change in z.

7 Some Further Issues

Most manuals on CBA provides only evaluation rules for small or marginal policy changes. The theoretical underpinnings often seem unclear. Do they consider marginal projects in the mathematical sense or are the rules rough approximations, perhaps based on textbook treatments? Apparently, the scale of a project may have a tremendous impact on how to evaluate it. The study by Dietz and Hepburn (2013) makes this obvious. The current section adds to the study by Dietz and Hepburn by deriving three different cost–benefit rules. The major rule derived in Section 7.1 is designed so as to handle large projects. Reducing project size, in the limit as it goes to zero we arrive at a truly marginal evaluation rule. The third rule draws on a linear approximation, but we claim that the rule is applicable also to quite large projects. Using data from two Swedish studies of green certificates, we are able to illustrate how the different measures perform. This is done in Section 7.2. Also in the case of the value of (a statistical) life, considered in Section 7.3, there is marginal versus nonmarginal issue. The conventional measure is problematic when risk changes not are infinitesimally small. Finally, we consider briefly how to undertake sensitivity analysis. Both deterministic analysis, Section 7.4 and robustness checks, Section 7.5, based on stochastic tools are considered.

The reader is informed that this section is more challenging from a technical/mathematical point of view than the rest of this Element.

7.1   *Three Cost–Benefit Rules: Point Estimates versus More Flexible Approaches*

In deriving our cost–benefit rules, we set aside distributional issues. Therefore, there is just a single, representative household in the economy and we focus on a single period to avoid unnecessary notational clutter. The indirect utility function of this household serves as the social welfare function:

$$V = V(p^f, p^{Af}, \pi + \pi^A + m^L) = V(p^f, p^{Af}, m), \qquad (7.1)$$

where $p^f = (1+\tau) \cdot p$, denotes the consumer price of x, the commodity of interest here, p denotes the producer price, τ is an ad valorem tax, all other commodities (except the numéraire) are aggregated into a single composite commodity, x^A, with consumer price denoted p^{Af}, π denotes profit income earned by the representative firm producing x, π^A denotes profits earned by the representative firm supplying x^A, and m^L denotes a lump-sum (tax) revenue.

Suppose the ad valorem tax is altered, affecting welfare. The resulting compensating variation is implicitly defined by the following equation:

$$V(p^{f1}, p^{Af1}, m^1 - CV) = V(p^{f0}, p^{Af0}, m^0), \qquad (7.2)$$

where a superscript 0 (1) refers to the initial (final) general equilibrium levels of relative prices. In order to focus on the taxed commodity, it is assumed that the shift in the tax only marginally affects the price of the composite commodity. Therefore, as shown in Section 3.1, the welfare effects of any change in p^{Af} sum to zero.

Next, let us solve Eq. (7.2) for CV and provide both an exact measure and a useful approximation that is easier to estimate in empirical applications:

$$CV = -\int_{p^{f0}}^{p^{f1}} h(.)dp^f + \varDelta\pi + \varDelta m^L \approx -[2 \cdot x^0 + \varDelta x]\frac{\varDelta p_t^f}{2} + \varDelta m,$$

$$(7.3)$$

where $h(.)$ refers to a Hicksian demand function, the WTP/WTA for a change in lump-sum income equals the change itself, and in the right- hand side expression a linear Marshallian consumer surplus measure is used to approximate the Hicksian WTP/WTA. The consumer surplus triangle plus the change in consumer surplus on the initial units reduce to the rule of half. There are several properties of Eq. (7.3) that deserves mentioning. First of all, $CV \cdot \overline{V}_m = \varDelta V$, where $\overline{V}_m > 0$ is the marginal utility of income evaluated at some $m \in [m^0, m^1 - CV]$. Thus, CV is a sign-preserving measure of the underlying change in utility. Second, the middle expression is a line integral. Thus, each change is evaluated conditional on all previous changes, that is, the household is throughout kept at its initial level of welfare. Third, the linear measure in (7.3) is exact if the utility function is quasi-linear and the demand function for x is linear; refer to Johansson and Kriström (2017a). CV is a variation of Harberger's (1971) deadweight loss triangle.

In the limit as $\Delta\tau$ goes to zero, Eq. (7.3) reduces to:

$$dCV = -x^0 dp^f + x^0 dp + [x^0(\tau dp + p d\tau) + p \cdot \tau dx] = p \cdot \tau dx,$$

$$(7.4)$$

where, as before, x^0 denotes the initial general equilibrium quantity of the commodity, the second term in the middle expression denotes the change in producer surplus, and the terms within brackets sum to dm^L. In the limit, if there is no taxation, the consumer surplus change caused by a marginal change in the price is equal to the negative of the producer surplus change of the same price change. The single remaining term in the right-hand side of the equation captures the extra deadweight loss caused by an increase in the tax rate. If the composite commodity is subject to an ad valorem tax, one would have to add a term similar to the final one to the equation.

Equation (7.4) provides a general equilibrium cost–benefit rule for an infinitesimally small policy change. The rule need not be seriously erroneous if applied to nonmarginal policies. It provides a reasonable approximation of CV whenever the changes in consumer and producer surpluses more or less cancel out. However, it is possible to arrive at a more precise empirical estimate of arbitrary-sized projects by undertaking a particular linear approximation around the initial level of utility:

$$\frac{V(p^{f1}, y + \pi^1 + m^{L1})}{V_m^0} - \frac{V(p^{f0}, y + \pi^0 + m^{L0})}{V_m^0} =$$

$$\frac{\Delta V}{V_m^0} \approx - [x^0(.) \cdot \Delta p^f - \Delta\pi - \Delta m^L],$$

$$(7.5)$$

where V_m^0 is the marginal utility of income evaluated at initial income, and the composite sector's profit income is suppressed. The first term within brackets in the second line of Eq. (7.5) is Roy's Identity, that is, the negative of the derivative of the indirect utility function with respect to the consumer price of x divided by the partial derivative of the indirect utility function with respect to income, multiplied by the change in the consumer price. The approach in Eq. (7.5) exploits all available information with respect to changes in profit income and tax income, but for a sufficiently small policy change it reduces to the measure in Eq. (7.4).

7.2 How do the Rules Perform? An Empirical Illustration

The study by Johansson and Kriström (2017) evaluates a scrapping of the Swedish green certificate scheme. The scheme is there to promote electricity produced by renewable sources. Consumers are required to buy certificates for a proportion of their electricity. These certificates are traded in the market and generate income for green power plants in addition to the spot price of electricity. Suppose the certificates are scrapped. Based on numbers in Johansson and Kriström (2017) x^0 is 90 TWh, Δx is 1.20673 TWh, the certificate price is SEK 0.16/kWh, and Δp^f = -0.0462/kWh.[22] The quota, denoted α, is assumed to be 0.231 as in 2016; SEK 10.77 = GBP 1 on October 21, 2017.

For the nonmarginal measures, the consumer surplus change (CS) of phasing out the certificate system is estimated as specified in Eqs. (7.3) and (7.5). Thus, the consumer surplus change in Eq. (7.3) is approximated by the linear measure; integrating the negative of an isoelastic demand function between initial and final end user prices, calibrated on Swedish data, and assuming the

---

[22] $p^f = (p^s + \alpha \cdot p^c + \tau^e + p^d) \cdot (1 + \tau^m)$, where $p^s = 0.26$ denotes the spot price per kWh, α denotes the quota, $p^c = 0.16$ denotes the certificate price, $\tau^e = 0.23$ denotes an average unit tax, $p^d = 0.3$ denotes the variable transmission tariff, and $\tau^m = 0.25$ denotes the value added tax. The total initial tax rate when $\alpha = 0.231$ is $\tau^0 = 0.43674$ and the total tax for $\alpha = 0$ is $\tau^1 = 0.4275$.

Table 7.1 Comparison of three different evaluation
rules, where *CS* refers to consumer surplus. Billion SEK.

Measure	Eq. (7.3)	Eq. (7.4)[a]	Eq. (7.5)
CS	4.186	3.326	4.158
$\Delta\pi$	-3.326	—	-3.326
Δm^L	-0.316	0.527	-0.316
Σ	0.544	3.853	0.516

[a] Plus $CS = -x^0 \cdot p^c \Delta\alpha$.

income effect is about zero as econometric evidence suggest, produces the same consumer surplus change as the linear approximation in Eq. (7.3). The estimates are reported in Table 7.1.
Note that we can approximate the *CS*-area by an outer rectangle,
i.e., $(x^0 + \Delta x)\Delta p^f$ (SEK 4.21 billion), and an inner rectangle,
i.e., $x^0 \Delta p^f$ (SEK 4.16 billion). The loss in profit income as the
certificates are phased out is estimated as $\Delta\pi = \Delta\alpha \cdot 0.16 \cdot x^0$; marginal
capacity on the Nordic spot market supplying Δx is assumed to set
price equal to marginal cost. There is a loss of value added tax
income on x^0 but a gain on Δx.[23] Environmental effects are ignored
because they coincide for the evaluation approaches.

The point-estimate or marginal rule will differ from the one in
Eq. (7.4), because a change in the quota in addition has a demand
effect (not found on the supply side) that must be accounted for; refer
to Johansson et al. (2017) for details. The associated consumer
surplus gain is obtained by multiplying initial demand x^0 by SEK
0.16·0.231 ($= -x^0 \cdot p^c \Delta\alpha$). The effects of any change in profit income
sums to zero, as discussed in Section 3.1. The change in tax income is
positive, because the measure values the total tax rate ($\tau = 0.43674$)
against the increase in electricity demand; refer to Eq. (7.4).

According to Table 7.1 the strictly marginal measure performs
poorly. The measure causes an overestimation of the social gain of
phasing out the certificates by a factor seven. The linear

---

[23] $\Delta m^L = (\tau^1 - \tau^0) \cdot x^0 + \tau^1 \Delta x = \Delta\alpha \cdot 0.16 \cdot 0.25 \cdot x^0 + 0.4275 \cdot \Delta x$.

approximation in Eq. (7.5) performs much better, because it is based on the same changes in profits and tax income as Eq. (7.3). The approximation of the consumer surplus is quite accurate. The overall error in comparison to Eq. (7.3) is just around six percent.

It may seem improper to apply the strictly marginal measure to a nonmarginal change. Therefore, let us briefly compare the measures if the quota is increased by one tenth of a percentage point (from 23.1 to 23.2 percent). Johansson et al. (2017) estimate that the price increase is SEK 0.0002 per kWh and that consumption deceases by 5.2 GWh. The reported loss of consumer surplus is SEK 14.4 million and the loss of tax revenue SEK 2.3 million. Applying the two nonmarginal measures to the same policy change produces a loss of no more than SEK 2.2 million: the loss of consumer surplus is around SEK 18 million, the gain in producer surplus is SEK 14.4 million, and the tax gain amounts to SEK 1.4 million. The point estimate in Eq. (7.4) multiplies the tax by the negative change in electricity consumption, explaining the loss of tax revenue, while the two other measures evaluate the total change in tax revenue.

Measures like the one in Eq. (7.4) are correct in the limit as project size goes to zero. Nevertheless, the comparison undertaken in this section underscores the importance of trying to use flexible approximations when deriving cost–benefit rules to be used to assess reasonably (but not infinitesimally) small projects. The lesson learned is that seemingly elegant and exact cost–benefit rules could be problematic to apply on real world policy measures. Our findings add to the concerns raised by Dietz and Hepburn (2013). In addition, there is a second-best element involved that deserves mentioning. Phasing-out the certificates, causes a loss of income. In turn, this income loss reduces demand for other commodities, causing a loss of value-added tax income in the rest of the economy. Moreover, the increase in electricity demand is expected to increase harmful emissions.

7.3　On the Value of a Statistical Life

The VSL, often also referred to as the value of preventing a fatality (VPF), is typically defined as the WTP for an infinitesimally small mortality risk reduction divided by the mortality risk reduction. Strictly speaking, it is the marginal rate of substitution, *MRS*, of income for mortality risk, that is, the absolute value of the slope of an indifference curve evaluated at a particular "point", as is shown in Figure 6; refer to Rosen (1988). This procedure standardizes the WTP so that it refers to a single (anonymous) life.

In stated-preference studies mortality risk reductions cannot be infinitesimally small if one aims at meaningful answers. By definition infinitesimal is much smaller than the risks of 1 in 100 000 typically valued in recent stated-preference surveys, and which people hopefully can relate to if illustrated as e.g. a reduction from 10 to 9 black grid cells in a diagram of 100 000 cells or described as a reduction from 10 to 9 persons dying prematurely in a town of 100 000 people. Moreover, these risk reductions relate to a year or so, not to fractions of a second. Similarly, it is hard to see that markets would price infinitesimally small risk

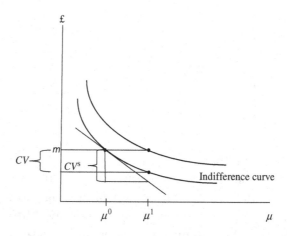

Figure 6 The WTP for a large risk reduction and a measure (denoted CV^S) based on the slope of the indifference curve.

changes. Moreover, as indicated below, empirical work indicates that VSL decreases as the magnitude of risk reduction is increased. This illustrates the importance of designing measures indicating how VSL behaves if changes in survival probabilities are not infinitesimally small. Some policy measures potentially cause very large changes in mortality risk. Evaluating new cures of previously untreatable diseases or the impact of climate change raises the question whether to evaluate actual changes in hazard rates or use *MRS*-based point estimates.

To shed some further light on these issues, consider an increase in the survivor probability of size $\Delta\mu = \mu^1 - \mu^0$. Denote an individual's WTP for this risk reduction *CV*. Then, the measure of the value of an (anonymous) life equals:

$$VSL = \frac{CV(m, \mu^0, \mu^1)}{\Delta\mu}. \tag{7.6}$$

To illustrate, suppose the average respondent is willing to pay £10 for a policy that is expected to reduce the number of fatal road accidents from 10 per 10^5 to 9 per 10^5 cars. Then the WTP for preventing a fatality is £10/(1/10^5) = $1 \cdot 10^6$ or £1 million. It can be shown that the *CV*-measure in Eq. (7.6) is increasing but at a decreasing rate in the magnitude of the risk reduction. Thus, doubling the magnitude of the risk reduction does not cause *CV* to double, as many health economists have assumed. Thus, *VSL* is *decreasing* in the magnitude of $\Delta\mu$. Moreover, drawing on l'Hôpital's rule it can be shown that *VSL* reduces to the *MRS* of income for mortality risk as $\Delta\mu \rightarrow 0$, that is, to the conventional definition of the VSL. The measure is sensitive not only to the magnitude of the risk change, but also to the magnitude of the (initial or) baseline risk. Refer to the Appendix for technical details.

Figure 6 provides an illustration. The conventional measure, based on the absolute value of the slope of the indifference curve and denoted CV^s in the figure is incorrect unless $\Delta\mu \rightarrow 0$, that is, unless we make a point-estimate, or indifference curves are linear; *VSL* decreases in the figure because the *MRS* decreases as μ and

$\Delta\mu$ increases. The conventional measure provides an *upper bound* for the *VSL*-measure in Eq. (7.6). If one considers a risk increase, the outcome is reversed. Now, the conventional measure provides a *lower bound* for the *VSL*-measure. This can be seen by noting that indifference curves become steeper as the survivor probability is reduced in Figure 6. A simple illustration is provided by $\Delta V^E = \mu^1 \cdot (m - CV)^{(1/2)} - \mu^0 \cdot m^{(1/2)} = 0$, resulting in $VSL = CV/\Delta\mu = m \cdot [1 - (\mu^0/\mu^1)^2]/\Delta\mu$. It is easily verified that this measure is increasing in income (or GDP/capita) and in the initial survivor probability, decreasing (increasing) in the magnitude of $\Delta\mu$ if $\Delta\mu > 0$ ($\Delta\mu < 0$), and reduces to $MRS = 2 \cdot m/\mu^0$ as $\mu^1 \to \mu^0$.

Finally, let us provide some empirical evidence. Lindhjem et al. (2011) present the first worldwide meta-regression analysis of stated-preference VSL-estimates. They find that VSL is decreasing in the magnitude of $\Delta\mu$.[24] In a meta-regression analysis of the VSL in road safety, de Blaeij et al. (2003) records the same pattern. A negative relationship is also found in hedonic wage studies. Refer to figure 4.6 in Viscusi (2015, p. 98). Qualitatively, these results are as predicted by Eq. (7.6).

7.4 Sensitivity Analysis

A one-way sensitivity analysis varies one parameter at a time. If the best estimate is used in the base-case CBA the investigator might be able to locate extreme values in a plausible range of the parameter and use these in the sensitivity analysis. Alternatively, it might be possible to construct a confidence interval (say, 95 percent) for the parameter. If a value or range for the parameter cannot be found, perform a threshold analysis: the parameter is assigned a value such that the outcome of the CBA takes on a chosen value, for example, shows a zero result.

---

[24] $VSL = e^{[a\overline{X} + b\ln(\Delta\mu)]}$, i.e., $\partial VSL/\partial(\Delta\mu) = b \cdot e^{a\overline{X}} \cdot (\Delta\mu)^{b-1} < 0$, where $a\overline{X}$ is a shortcut for the average impact of all other significant factors and $b < 0$ is a regression coefficient; b is significant ($p < 0.01$ or $p < 0.05$) in 18 of 19 regressions.

To undertake a single univariate sensitivity analysis does not make much sense. In the more reasonable case, multiple univariate sensitivity analyses are undertaken. Instead of presenting the intervals in a table they are often presented in a Tornado diagram: the parameters are ordered according to their impact on the result from widest range to most narrow range.

Sometimes we must undertake multivariate sensitivity analyses. For example, parameters might be correlated so that their total impact is larger or smaller than the sum of their impact according to univariate analyses. In the simplest case, we consider two-way sensitivity analysis where two parameters are varied at a time. A typical approach is to construct a diagram in which the two parameters are varied so as to keep the result unchanged, constructing a type of indifference curves or isoquants where each curve keeps the result at a particular level. However, it is unlikely that both parameters take on their extreme values together. Therefore, try to find a set of parameter values that provide a likely upper bound and a lower bound, respectively, for the outcome.

7.5   Risk Analysis

The *stochastic* approach to sensitivity analysis, often termed risk analysis, takes a different view of the basic problem. It treats the vector of basic parameters as a stochastic variable with a given distribution. This approach where probability distributions are assumed for different parameters has recently become popular. Johansson and Kriström (2012) establish what they term cost–benefit acceptability curves as they yield the probability that the social profitability exceeds, say, £x million. Such curves could turn out to be useful for decision makers because they give the likelihood of success of a project as well as the odds that it passes any "security" margin the decision maker would like to add. Such curves can be estimated using either assumed probability distributions for different parameters or Monte Carlo simulation techniques.

One such case is shown in Figure 7. It is taken from a CBA of a reregulation of a Swedish river. Refer to Johansson and Kriström

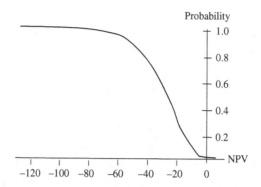

Figure 7 A cost–benefit acceptability curve.

(2012). Given the base-case estimate, which is SEK –32 million, and the reasonable lower and upper bounds for the outcome (–124 and 7, respectively), a distribution that fits the data reasonably well and is able to generate a mean equal to –32 is the Gumbel (minimum) or extreme value type I distribution. It has the following survivor function:

$$G(x) = e^{-e^{(x-l)/s}} \tag{7.7}$$

where s is a scale parameter, set equal to 14, and l is a location parameter, set equal to –24. The cost–benefit acceptability curve is traced out by letting x run from minus infinity to plus infinity in the survivor function.

The distribution in Figure 7 is obviously very skewed (preventing the use of, e.g., a triangular or even the more general trapezoidal distribution as they are unable to generate a mean of –32 given the assumed range [–124, 7]). Moreover the probability that the project breaks even or earns a positive surplus is virtually nil.

A refinement would be to explicitly assume probability distributions for each of the involved variables. However, the multivariate probability density and distribution functions easily become virtually impossible to handle when there are many and possibly not independent random variables. Therefore, some kind of numerical approach is needed. Monte Carlo methods provide approximate solutions to a variety of mathematical problems by performing statistical sampling experiments. There are many different Monte Carlo methods since there are many different ways of approximating, say, a complex integral. In any case, the idea behind a Monte Carlo simulation is to sample values of key parameters from their assumed distributions. For example, the discount rate might be assumed to be drawn from a (truncated) normal distribution, a price variable from a uniform distribution, a cost item from a triangular distribution, and so on. Then, calculate a net present value, given the drawn numbers. By repeating this process a large number of times, a distribution of net present values is obtained, showing how sensitive the project is to stochastically perturbing the key parameters. This approach is more flexible than the one in Eq. (7.7) because the simulation approach allows use of a distribution for each key parameter rather than a single one for the "aggregate" and individual distributions are allowed to be interrelated.

It is not necessarily true that this approach generates the same expected NPV as the base-case CBA. To see why, consider the case with two stochastic variables with expected values x^E and y^E. The expected value of the product of x and y is not equal to $x^E \cdot y^E$ unless the two variables are independent: $E(xy) = x^E \cdot y^E + \text{cov}(x, y)$. It is important to be aware of this issue when undertaking sensitivity analysis based on correlated stochastic variables. If distributions are known, the ideal candidate for the base-case CBA would be $E[\text{NPV}(\Omega)]$, where Ω is a vector of stochastic as well as non-stochastic variables, that is, all variables affecting the considered project's net present value; $E[\text{NPV}(\Omega)]$ may exceed or fall short of CBA based on expected parameter values (that is, $\text{NPV}(\Omega^E)$). The problem is that the distributions are not known, in general. Sometimes they must be based on quite arbitrary assumptions, but in other cases the distributions of stochastic variables can be based on reasonable procedures for eliciting beliefs or inference from the available information set, not differently from forecasting in several other areas of economics, engineering, and other sciences.

Monte Carlo techniques share many similarities to resampling methods such as bootstrap and jackknife (and sometimes resampling methods are referred to as a type of Monte Carlo simulation). In Monte Carlo techniques, we sample randomly from known/ assumed distributions. In resampling methods, the simulated samples are drawn from an existing sample of data. The data is taken to be the population, and sampling with replacement is used. The fundamental idea is that the data arise as a sample from some probability distribution. For example, if a sample of people is asked for their WTP for a policy, bootstrap methods can be used to estimate confidence intervals. Thus, both of these techniques are relevant for CBA.

Appendix: Some Properties of the VSL Measure

The expected utility function behind the results in Section 7.3 is defined as follows:

$$V^E = \mu \cdot V(m - CV), \tag{A.1}$$

where all arguments but disposable income are suppressed, and $CV = 0$ initially. The VSL measure associated with a change in the survivor probability from μ^0 to μ^1 is defined as follows:

$$VSL_{\mu^0,\,\mu^1,\,m} = \frac{CV(m,\mu^0,\mu^1)}{\Delta\mu}. \tag{A.2}$$

Let us examine the impact on *VSL* of a marginal change in the "with policy" survivor rate μ^1 (with $\mu^1 > \mu^0$):

$$\frac{\partial VSL}{\partial \mu^1} = \frac{\partial CV(.)/\partial \mu^1}{\Delta\mu} - \frac{CV}{(\Delta\mu)^2} = \frac{1}{\Delta\mu}[\partial CV(.)/\partial\mu^1 - \frac{CV}{\Delta\mu}]$$

$$= \frac{1}{\Delta\mu}[MRS_{\mu^1,m-CV} - VSL] < 0. \tag{A.3}$$

In Figure 6, $\partial CV(.)/\partial\mu^1$ is the negative of the slope of the indifference curve at $(\mu^1, m - CV)$, i.e., equals $MRS_{\mu^1,m-CV}(< MRS_{\mu^0,m}$ used to define CV^s in the figure). If $\mu^1 > \mu^0$, then $(\partial CV/\partial\mu^1)\Delta\mu < CV$. In terms of Figure 6, the indifference curve becomes flatter and flatter as we move from μ^0 toward μ^1. Therefore, a measure based on the slope at $(\mu^1, m - CV)$ must be smaller than CV, implying that $MRS_{\mu^1,m-CV} < CV/\Delta\mu = VSL$. Thus, $\partial VSL/\partial\mu^1 < 0$. The same holds if $\mu^1 < \mu^0$, because now $MRS_{\mu^1,m-CV} > CV/\Delta\mu = VSL$ while CV, $\Delta\mu < 0$. These results imply that reducing μ^1, with $\mu^1 \neq \mu^0$, increases *VSL*.

If $\mu^1 = \mu^0$ Eq. (7.6) reduces to the indeterminate expression $0/0$. However, taking partial derivatives of the numerator and the denominator with respect to μ^1 and evaluating these at $\mu^1 = \mu^0$, i.e., applying l'Hôpital's rule, one obtains:

$$VSL_{\mu^0,\,m} = \frac{\partial CV(.)/\partial \mu^1}{1} = MRS_{\mu^0,\,m}. \tag{A.4}$$

References

Arrow, K. J., Cropper, M. L., Gollier, C., et al. (2014). Should governments use a declining discount rate in project analysis? *Review of Environmental Economics and Policy*, **8**, 145–163.

Arrow, K. J., Cropper, M. L., Gollier, C., et al. (2012). How should benefits and costs be discounted in an intergenerational context? Resources for the Future Discussion Paper 12-53, Washington, DC, www.rff.org/RFF/Documents/RFF-DP-12-53.pdf.

Arrow, K. J., & Fisher, A. C. (1974). Environmental preservation, uncertainty, and irreversibility. *Quarterly Journal of Economics*, **88**, 312–319.

Arrow, K., Solow, R., Portney, P. R., et al. (1993). Report of the NOAA Panel on contingent valuation. *Federal Register*, **58**, 4601–4614.

Ayer, M., Brunk, H. D., Ewing, G. M., Reid, W. T., & Silverman, E. (1955). An empirical distribution function for sampling with incomplete information. *The Annals of Mathematical Statistics*, **26**, 641–647.

Ballard, C. L., & Fullerton, D. (1992). Distortionary taxation and the provision of public goods. *Journal of Economic Perspectives*, **6**, 117–131.

Barro, R. J., & Grossman, H. I. (1976). *Money, Employment and Inflation*, Cambridge: Cambridge University Press.

Becker, G. S. (1960). An economic analysis of fertility. In Roberts, G. B., ed., *Demographic and Economic Change in Developed Countries*, Princeton, NJ: Princeton University Press, pp. 209–240.

Belyaev, Y., & Kriström, B. (2015). Analysis of survey data containing rounded censoring intervals. *Informatics and Applications*, **9**, 2–10.

Blackorby, C., & Donaldson, D. (1990). A review article: The case against the use of the sum of compensating variations in cost-benefit analysis. *Canadian Journal of Economics*, **23**, 471–494.

Blanchard, O. J., & Fisher, S. (1996). *Lectures on Macroeconomics*, Cambridge, MA: The MIT Press.

Boadway, R. (2017). Second-best theory: Ageing well at sixty. *Pacific Economic Review*, **22**, 249–270.

Boadway, R. (1975). Cost-benefit rules in general equilibrium. *Review of Economic Studies*, **42**, 361–374.

87

Boadway, R. W. (1974). The welfare foundations of cost-benefit analysis. *Economic Journal*, **84**, 926–939.

Boadway, R. W., & Bruce, N. (1984). *Welfare Economics*, Oxford: Basil Blackwell.

Botzen, W. W. J., & van den Bergh, J. C. J. M. 2014. Specifications of social welfare in economic studies of climate policy: Overview of criteria and related policy insights. *Environmental and Resource Economics*, **58**, 1–33.

Boyle, G., & Irwin, T. (2004). *A Primer on Real Options*, Wellington: New Zealand Institute for the Study of Competition and Regulation.

Carson, R. T. (2012). *Contingent Valuation: A Comprehensive Bibliography and History*, Cheltenham: Edward Elgar.

Carson, R. T., & Groves, T. (2011). Incentive and information properties of preference questions: Commentary and extensions. In Bennett, J., ed., *The International Handbook on Non-Market Environmental Valuation*, Northampton, MA: Edward Elgar, pp. 300–321.

Carson, R. T., & Groves, T. (2007). Incentive and informational properties of preference questions. *Environmental and Resource Economics*, **37**, 181–210.

Chay, K. Y., & Greenstone, M. (2005). Does air quality matter? Evidence from the housing market. *Journal of Political Economy*, **113**, 376–424.

Coelli, T., Lloyd-Smith, J., Morrison, D., & Thomas, J. (1991). Hedonic pricing for a cost benefit analysis of a public water supply scheme. *The Australian Journal of Agricultural Economics*, **35**, 1–20.

Cuddington, J. T., Johansson, P.-O., & Löfgren, K.-G. (1984). *Disequilibrium Macroeconomics in Open Economies*, Oxford: Basil Blackwell.

Dahlby, B. (2008). *The Marginal Cost of Public Funds. Theory and Applications*, Cambridge, MA: The MIT Press.

de Blaeij, A., Florax, R. J. G. M., Rietveld, P., & Verhoef, E. (2003). The value of statistical life in road safety: A meta-analysis. *Accident Analysis and Prevention*, **35**, 973–986.

de Rus, G. (2010). *Introduction to Cost-Benefit Analysis. Looking for Reasonable Shortcuts*, Cheltenham: Edward Elgar.

Dietz, S., & Hepburn, C. (2013). Benefit–cost analysis of non-marginal climate and energy projects. *Energy Economics*, **40**, 61–71.

Dixit, A. K., & Pindyck, R. S. (1994). *Investment under Uncertainty*, Princeton, NJ: Princeton University Press.

Dolan, P., & Tsuchiya, A. (2011). Determining the parameters in social welfare function using stated preference data: An application to health. *Applied Economics*, **42**, 2241–2250.

Drèze, J., & Stern, N. (1987). The Theory of Cost–Benefit Analysis. In Auerbach, A. and M. Feldstein, eds., *Handbook in Public Economics*, Vol. II, Amsterdam: North-Holland, pp. 909–990.

Dupuit, J. (1849). De l'influence des péages sur l'utilité des voies de communication. *Annales des Ponts et Chaussées*, **207**, 170–248.

Eppen, G. D., Gould, F. J., & Schmidt, C. P. (1993). *Introductory Management Science*, 4th edn., Englewood Cliffs, NJ: Prentice-Hall International.

European Commission. (2014). *Guide to Cost–Benefit Analysis of Investment Projects: Economic Appraisal Tool for Cohesion Policy 2014–2020*, Brussels: Tech. rept. DG Regional Policy.

Fisher, A. C., & Hanemann, M. W. (1987). Quasi-option value: Some misconceptions dispelled. *Journal of Environmental Economics and Management*, **14**, 183–190.

Florio, M. (2014). *Applied Welfare Economics. Cost–Benefit Analysis of Projects and Policies*, New York: Routledge.

Florio, M., Forte, S., & Sirtori, E. (2016). Forecasting the socio-economic impact of the Large Hadron Collider: A cost–benefit analysis to 2025 and beyond. *Technological Forecasting and Social Change*, **112**, 38–53.

Freeman III, A. M., Heriges, J. A., & Kling, C. L. (2014). *The Measurement of Environmental and Resource Values. Theories and Methods*, 3rd edn., New York: RFF Press.

Gahvari, F. (2006). On the marginal cost of public funds and the optimal provision of public goods. *Journal of Public Economics*, **90**, 1251–1262.

Gollier, C., & Weitzman, M. L. (2010). How should the distant future be discounted when discount rates are uncertain? *Economics Letters*, **107**, 350–353.

Graham, D. A. (1981). Cost-benefit analysis under uncertainty. *American Economic Review*, 715–725.

Griliches, Z. (ed.). (1971). *Price Indexes and Quality Change*, Cambridge, MA: Harvard University Press.

Gustafsson, A., Herrmann, A., & Huber, F. (eds.) (2007). *Conjoint Measurement. Methods and Applications*, 4th edn., Heidelberg: Springer Verlag.

Harberger, A. C. (1971). Three basic postulates for applied welfare economics: An interpretive essay. *Journal of Economic Literature*, **9**, 785–797.

Harrison, M. (2010). Valuing the future: The social discount rate in cost-benefit analysis. Visiting Researcher Paper, Productivity Commission, Canberra, AUS, http://papers.ssrn.com/sol3/papers.cfm?abstract/ id=1599963.

Henry, C. (1974). Investment decisions under uncertainty: The irreversibility effect. *American Economic Review*, **64**, 1006–1012.

Hicks, J. R. (1939). The foundations of welfare economics. *The Economic Journal*, **49**, 696–712.

HM Treasury. (2011). *The Green Book. Appraisal and Evaluation in Central Government*, London: HMSO.

Hotelling, H. (1949). Letter of June 18, 1947, to Newton B. Drury. Tech. rep., Included in the report The Economics of Public Recreation: An Economic Study of the Monetary Evaluation of Recreation in the National Parks.

Jehle, G. A., & Reny, P. J. (2011). *Advanced Microeconomic Theory*, 3rd edn., Harlow: Financial Times Prentice Hall.

Johansson, P.-O. (1982). Cost–benefit rules in general disequilibrium. *Journal of Public Economics*, **18**, 121–137.

Johansson, P.-O., & Kriström, B. (2017). General equilibrium welfare evaluation in the small and in the large: Application to green certificate schemes. Mimeo.

Johansson, P.-O., & Kriström, B. (2017a). Rule of half as the outcome of utility maximization. Mimeo.

Johansson, P.-O., & Kriström, B. (2016). *Cost-Benefit Analysis for Project Appraisal*, Cambridge: Cambridge University Press.

Johansson, P.-O., & Kriström, B. (2015). On the social cost of water-related disasters. *Water Economics and Policy*, **1** (https://doi.org/10.1142/ S2382624X15500150).

Johansson, P. O., & Kriström, B. (2012). *The Economics of Evaluating Water Projects. Hydroelectricity versus Other Uses*. Heidelberg: Springer Verlag.

Johansson, P.-O., Kriström, B., & Böhringer, C. (2017). General equilibrium welfare evaluation of green certificate schemes in the small. Mimeo.

Johnston, R. J., Boyle, K. J., Ademowicz, W., et al. (2017). Contemporary guidance for stated preference studies. *Journal of the Association of Environmental and Resource Economists*, **4**, 319–405.

Jorge-Calderón, D., & Johansson, P.-O. (2017). Emissions trading and taxes: An application to airport investment appraisals. *Journal of Transport Economics and Policy*, **51**, 249–265.

Just, R. E., Hueth, D. L., & Schmitz, A. (2004). *The Welfare Economics of Public Policy: A Practical Approach to Project and Policy Evaluation*, Cheltenham: Edward Elgar.

Kaldor, N. (1939). Welfare propositions of economics and interpersonal comparisons of utility. *The Economic Journal*, **49**, 549–552.

Knight, F. H. (1921). *Risk, Uncertainty, and Profit*, Boston, MA: Houghton and Mifflin.

Kriström, B., & Johansson, P.-O. (2015). Economic valuation methods for non-market goods or services. In Wohl, E., ed., *Oxford Bibliographies in Environmental Science*, New York: Oxford University Press. DOI:10.1093/OBO/9780199363445-0044.

Kriström, B., & Laitila, T. (2003). Choice experiments: A user's guide. In Folmer, H. and T. Tietenberg, eds., *Yearbook of Environmental and Resource Economics*, Cheltenham: Edward Elgar, pp. 305–330.

Lancaster, K. (1971). *Consumer Demand: A New Approach*, New York: Columbia University Press.

Lancaster, K. (1966). A new approach to consumer theory. *Journal of Political Economy*, **74**, 132–157.

Lesourne, J. (1975). *Cost–Benefit Analysis and Economic Theory*, Amsterdam: North-Holland.

Lesourne, J. (1972). *Le Calcul Économique: Théorie et Applications*, 2nd edn., Paris: Dunod.

Lindhjem, H., Navrud, S., Braathen, N. A., & Biausque, V. (2011). Valuing mortality risk reductions from environmental, transport, and health policies: A global meta-analysis of stated preference studies. *Risk Analysis*, **31**, 1381–1407.

Loureiro, M. L., & Loomis, J. B. (2013). International public preferences and provision of public goods: Assessment of passive use values in large oil spills. *Environmental and Resource Economics*, **56**, 521–534.

Louviere, J. J., Flynn, T. N., & Carson, R. T. (2010). Discrete choice experiments are not conjoint analysis. *Journal of Choice Modelling*, **3**, 57–72.

Luce, R. D., & Tukey, J. W. (1964). Simultaneous conjoint measurement: A new type of fundamental measurement. *Journal of Mathematical Psychology*, **1**, 1–27.

Mahieu, P.-A., Riera, P., Kriström, B., Brännlund, R., & Giergiczny, M. (2014). Exploring the determinants of uncertainty in contingent valuation surveys. *Journal of Environmental Economics and Policy*, **3**, 186–200.

Mäler, K.-G. (2002). Are social welfare functions ordinal or cardinal? Beijer Discussion Paper Series No. 148, Stockholm: The Beijer Institute of Ecological Economics.

Mäler, K.-G. (1985). Welfare Economics and the Environment. In Kneese, A. V. and J. L. Sweeney, eds., *Handbook of Natural Resource and Energy Economics*, vol. 1, Amsterdam: North-Holland, pp. 3–60.

Mäler, K.-G. (1974). *Environmental Economics: A Theoretical Inquiry*. Baltimore, MD: Johns Hopkins University Press for Resources for the Future.

McAllister, P. H., Stone, J. C., & Dantzig, G. B. (1989). Deriving a utility function for the U.S. economy. Journal of Policy Modeling, 11, 391–429.

Mensink, P., & Requate, T. (2005). The Dixit–Pindyck and the Arrow-Fisher-Hanemann-Henry option values are not equivalent: A note on Fisher (2000). *Resource and Energy Economics*, **27**, 83–88.

Milgrom, P. (1993). Is sympathy an economic value? Philosophy, economics and the contingent valuation method. In Hausman, J. A., ed., Contingent Valuation: A Critical Assessment, Amsterdam: Elsevier, pp. 417–435.

Myles, G. D. (1995). *Public Economics*, Cambridge: Cambridge University Press.

Palmquist, R. B. (2005). Weak complementarity, path independence, and the intuition of the Willig condition. *Journal of Environmental Economics and Management*, **49**, 103–115.

Pareto, V. (1896-1897). *Premier Cours d'Économie Politique Appliquée Professé à l'Université de Lausanne*, Paris: Rouge/Pichon.

Parsons, G. R. (2013). Travel cost methods. In Shogren, J. F., ed., *Encyclopedia of Energy, Natural Resource, and Environmental Economics*, Amsterdam: Elsevier, pp. 349–358.

Phelps, E. S., & Pollak, R. A. (1968). On second-best national saving and game-equilibrium growth. *Review of Economic Studies*, **35**, 185–199.

Quinet, É. (2013). *Cost benefit assessment of public investments. Final report. Summary and recommendations.* Paris: Commissariat general à la stratégie et à la prospective.

Robinson, L. A., & Hammitt, J. K. (2011). Behavioral economics and the conduct of benefit–cost analysis: Towards principles and standards. *Journal of Benefit-Cost Analysis*, **2**, (2), art. 5.

Rosen, S. (1988). The value of changes in life expectancy. *Journal of Risk and Uncertainty*, **1**, 285–304.

Rosen, S. (1974). Hedonic prices and implicit markets: Product differentiation in pure competition. *Journal of Political Economy*, **82**, 34–55.

Ruiz-Castillo, J. (1987). Potential welfare and the sum of individual compensating or equivalent variations. *Journal of Economic Theory*, **41**, 34–53.

Saez, E., & Stantcheva, S. (2016). Generalized social marginal welfare weights for optimal tax theory. *American Economic Review*, **106**, 24–45.

Smith, V. K. (1991). Household production functions and environmental benefit estimation. In Braden, J. B. and C. D. Kolstad, eds., *Measuring the Demand for Environmental Quality*, Amsterdam: North-Holland, pp. 41–76.

Smith, V. K., & Moore, E. M. (2010). Behavioral economics and benefit cost analysis. *Environmental and Resource Economics*, **46**, 217–234.

Stern, N. (2007). *The Economics of Climate Change. The Stern Review*, Cambridge: Cambridge University Press.

Stigler, S. M. (1980). Stigler's law of eponymy. *Transactions of the New York Academy of Sciences*, **39**, 147–157.

Strotz, R. H. (1955–1956). Myopia and Inconsistency in Dynamic Utility Maximization. *Review of Economic Studies*, **23**, 165–180.

Traeger, C. P. (2014). On option values in environmental and resource economics. *Resource and Energy Economics*, **37**, 242–252.

US EPA. (2010). *Guidelines for preparing economic analyses. U.S. Environmental Protection Agency (EPA)*, Updated May 2014, Washington, DC: EPA 240-R-00-003.

Viscusi, W. K. (2015). The heterogeneity of the value of statistical life: Evidence and policy implications. In Mansfield, C. and V. K. Smith, eds., *Benefit-Cost Analyses for Security Policies. Does Increased Safety Have to Reduce Efficiency?* Cheltenham: Edward Elgar, pp. 78–116.

Weimer, D. L. (2017). *Behavioral Economics for Cost-Benefit Analysis. Benefit Validity When Sovereign Consumers Seem to Make Mistakes.* Cambridge: Cambridge University Press.

Whittington, D., & MacRae, Jr.,D. (1986). The issue of standing in cost-benefit analysis. *Journal of Policy Analysis and Management*, **5**, 665–682.

Yunker, J. A. (1989). Some empirical evidence on the social welfare maximization hypothesis. *Public Finance*, **44**, 110–133.

Acknowledgements

We are grateful to the editors of the Cambridge Elements series in Public Economics, Professors Robin Boadway, Frank Cowell, and Massimo Florio, and the Associate Editor Dr. Chiara Del Bo for their generous support. Two anonymous reviewers provided us with detailed and very constructive comments. However, any remaining errors and other flaws are our own responsibility.

Cambridge Elements ☰

Public Economics

Robin Boadway
Queen's University
Robin Boadway is Emeritus Professor of Economics at Queen's University. His main research interests are in public economics, welfare economics and fiscal federalism.

Frank A. Cowell
The London School of Economics and Political Science
Frank A. Cowell is Professor of Economics at the London School of Economics. His main research interests are in inequality, mobility and the distribution of income and wealth.

Massimo Florio
University of Milan
Massimo Florio is Professor of Public Economics at the University of Milan. His main interests are in cost-benefit analysis, regional policy, privatization, public enterprise, network industries and the socio-economic impact of research infrastructures.

About the series
The Cambridge Elements of Public Economics provides authoritative and up-to-date reviews of core topics and recent developments in the field. It includes state-of-the-art contributions on all areas in the field. The editors are particularly interested in the new frontiers of quantitative methods in public economics, experimental approaches, behavioral public finance, empirical and theoretical analysis of the quality of government and institutions.

Cambridge Elements ≡

Public Economics

Elements in the series

Cost–Benefit Analysis
Per-Olav Johansson and Bengt Kriström

A full series listing is available at: www.cambridge.org/ElePubEcon

Printed in the United States
By Bookmasters